Forty Day Trips from Rota

Forty Day Trips from Rota

◆

Easy Adventures in Southern Spain

With Illustrations by Jim Ronka

Melinda Ronka

iUniverse, Inc.
New York Lincoln Shanghai

Forty Day Trips from Rota
Easy Adventures in Southern Spain

iUniverse books may be ordered through booksellers or by contacting:

iUniverse
2021 Pine Lake Road, Suite 100
Lincoln, NE 68512
www.iuniverse.com
1-800-Authors (1-800-288-4677)

ISBN: 0-595-34129-2

Printed in the United States of America

Contents

Introduction

Travel can be fun, adventurous, and educational. It *shouldn't* be frustrating, annoying, or irritating...but sometimes it is. *Forty Day Trips from Rota* is designed to help the independent traveler reduce some of the frustrations of travel by providing advice and tips for one-day trips in and around Andalucía. But before you start, here are some helpful hints about travels in Spain.

Most tourist attractions are closed on Mondays. *Siesta*, the afternoon rest period, lasts from 14:00 to 17:00, and you will find most stores and some tourist attractions closed during this time. Meal times are late compared to American standards. Many restaurants don't open until 14:00 for lunch and 20:00 for dinner, but you may be able to find food at a *venta*, a smaller restaurant, during off-hours.

Bring a good map. Driving directions are provided, but roads and landmarks can change. This book is *not* meant to take the place of a map or replace a more general guidebook. The maps provided here are designed to give you a general idea of where things are located.

Other guidebooks can provide you with more on Spanish history, hotel options, restaurants, and every museum possibility in a city. *Forty Day Trips from Rota* concentrates on what can be done in a day, hitting the highlights of a city but not every last detail. These city highlights, of course, are just suggestions. Feel free to explore each city on your own and make your own itinerary.

During our travels when we drove into a town, we preferred to park in a parking garage or pay lot over trying to find street parking, and that's how you are directed. While slightly more expensive, it's safer for your car that way.

Your first stop in a city should be the Tourist Information Office to pick up a map and information about the city. Most offices have a wealth of information and they're happy to share it with you.

Prices are provided for entry fees to tourist attractions to give you an idea of how expensive they are. These are listed as a very rough estimate, as fees are often increased yearly. If you're a local, and the ticket sales person asks where you're from, make sure to tell them your nationality but that you live here in Spain. Sometimes they will consider that to be good enough for a free European Union ticket. Many times we didn't have to pay the entry fee, but some times we did. It just depended on who was selling the tickets.

After each day trip listing, an area is provided for you to write down your travel experiences. Use it as a travel journal and record your experiences, your travel partners, what you saw, or what you ate. You will probably find your memories to be clearer and more vivid if you jot down a few notes, and it's a free souvenir of the place you visited.

While this book is written as day trip suggestions, I have a confession to make. We were traveling with a toddler, so if the travel time was over two and a half hours we often spent the night. In our travels, Antequera, Cordoba, Granada, Marbella, Morocco, and Portugal were weekend adventures. If weekend travel suits your taste, try www.Hotelclub.net and click on "Last Minute Deals" for great rates on local hotels.

Lastly, a word of caution…when we travel, we tend to exhaust our guests. These trips are ambitious, but a lot of fun. Wear good walking shoes and bring a good attitude. You'll have a great time exploring this unique and lovely part of Europe.

Antequera

When you visit Antequera and its outlying areas, you get a wide and varied look at this small corner of Spain. In the city of Antequera, you will find a traditional Moorish castle, large Catholic cathedral, and a smattering of Roman ruins. But venture out from the city center and you can see ancient tombs called dolmens and further on, El Torcal, a natural park featuring a lunar-like landscape. If you head out to Antequera, you can be assured you will experience a unique part of southern Spain.

Travel time: About two hours 15 minutes.

Things to do in a day:

    ❑   Make a donation and visit the Iglesia de Santa María. You can help support their work and go in and admire the pretty altar and domed ceiling. Besides, you probably parked in the plaza outside, so it's not like it's out of your way. Donation only. (Allow 15 minutes)

❑ Walk to the castle (it can be seen from the Iglesia de Santa María). In 2004 the interior was closed due to ongoing restoration, but you can walk through the Arco de los Gigantes (Arch of the Giants), ramble through the gardens, and scamper along the castle walls. When the restoration is complete, normal visiting hours should be Tuesday–Sunday from 10:00–14:00. (Allow 20–30 minutes)

❑ Walk to the cathedral, Real Colegiata de Santa María, located next to the castle. The church is from the Renaissance Period and has simpler lines than most of the Baroque churches you'll see in Spain. Don't miss the lovely wooden ceiling. Open on Tuesday–Friday from 10:30–14:00 and 16:30–18:30; Saturday from 10:30–14:00; and Sunday from 11:30–14:00. Closed Monday. Free. (Allow 20 minutes)

❑ Peek over the edge of the plaza next to the cathedral to see an excavation of Roman baths. (Five minutes)

❑ Drive to the dolmens. These tombs consist of huge, vertical blocks of stone supporting a slab stone ceiling. Considering the work was done during the Copper Age (2500–1800 BC), it's pretty impressive. You can visit both the Viera and Menga Dolmens in one stop. There will be a guide just inside the gate who will open up the tombs. Open on Tuesday from 9:00–15:30; Wednesday–Saturday from 9:00–18:00; and Sunday from 9:30–14:30. Closed Monday. Free. (Allow 20–30 minutes)

❑ Drive to El Torcal Natural Park. The park is located at the top of the foothills outside Antequera. The rocky landscape is full of interesting limestone formations that originated on the then ocean floor during the Jurassic Period. Stop by the visitor's center, open all year from 10:00–17:00, to get a little history on the area. Then, starting at the trailhead located across the parking lot from the visitor's center, walk out 100 meters to the *mirador* (lookout) for views of the countryside. The opposite side of the parking lot is the launching point for the green route, a 1.5 km walk around the upper Torcal area. It's rated a low to medium difficulty hike and takes around 35–45 minutes.

Expect to do some rock scrambling along the way as you check out this unique landscape. Free. (Take 1–2 hours to explore the park)

Food tips: You will probably be in Antequera long enough to need a bite to eat and a cool drink. For a refreshing drink, stop at Mesón Restaurante El Escribano located in the plaza outside the Real Colegiata de Santa María cathedral. It is conveniently located opposite the cathedral, and has pleasant outdoor tables.

If you are looking for a meal on the way to or from El Torcal, you will find a number of *ventas* lining the country road (C-3310). We tried Complejo Rural El Torcal de Antequera since they were enterprising enough to give us a brochure as we were leaving the El Torcal parking lot. As you return to Antequera from El Torcal, it should be the first *venta* on your left located at C-3310 Km 6. They offer a cafeteria and restaurant, and menus in English. We tried the spiced meat skewers, which were excellent. "Andres" runs the place with effusive friendliness. Along with camping sites, he also has a pool and offers summer promotions of a meal and a swim for a set price; kids get a discount. You can find them on the web at www.torcalrural.com.

Highlight: The limestone formations in El Torcal were really incredible, like nothing we've ever seen in the states, *and* we saw a wild mountain goat.

Lowlight: One long day made for a grumpy baby, grumpy baby, grumpy baby!

Sidelight: Fifteen miles (24 km) from Antequera and 12 miles (19 km) out of your way, lies La Laguna de Fuente de Piedra, a nature reserve protecting a salt-water lagoon and an important nesting ground for flamingos. There's a Visitor's Center, a *mirador* (lookout), and some dirt trails running next to the lagoon. I wouldn't necessarily add this side trip on to an already busy day, but if you *really* like flamingos you might consider cutting your day short in Antequera to visit the lagoon. The visitor's center is open on Tuesday from 10:00–13:00 and 18:00–20:00; Wednesday–Friday from 10:00–14:00 and 18:00–20:00; and Saturday, Sunday, and holidays from 10:00–20:00. Closed Monday. Free.

Hints:

1. Get to Antequera early and don't go on a Monday. Most tourist things close down at 14:00 and aren't open on Mondays.

2.   After seeing pictures of the snakes and tarantulas found in El Torcal, you'll wish you were wearing hiking boots.

3.   If you want a brochure about the dolmens or El Torcal Natural Park, visit Antequera's Tourist Information Office and ask for them specifically. Neither the dolmens nor the park had any brochures displayed for visitors to take.

Directions: From Rota, drive towards Jerez on the A-491. At the casino/water park traffic circle take the 2:00 exit towards El Portal (CA-201). In six miles (10 km), when the road comes to a 'T' at a traffic circle, turn right onto the A-381. In one mile (1.6 km), take the A-4 north to Sevilla. In three miles (five km), take the A-382 exit. Turn right towards Arcos de la Frontera. Follow the A-382 for about 98 miles (158 km). Take the road to Antequera. Drive 3.3 miles (5.3 km) to reach a large traffic circle with arches at the beginning of town. Go straight 0.5 miles (0.8 km) to reach the traffic circle with a fountain where the Tourist Information Office is located. To find parking, go straight about 0.1 miles (0.1 km), turn right at the 'T' intersection, and drive up the hill about 0.4 miles (0.6 km) to reach a plaza with parking outside a large church, Iglesia de Santa María, and a smaller chapel.

To reach the dolmens, head back down the hill to the traffic circle with the Tourist Information (TI) Office and take the 3:00 exit, passing the TI office on your right. Drive about 0.4 miles (0.6 km) and turn right following the signs to the dolmens. Drive 0.5 miles (0.8 km) to reach the dolmens on your left. There is a small dirt parking lot and off-street parking.

To reach El Torcal Natural Park, from the traffic circle with the arches at the beginning of town, drive straight towards the TI office about 0.1 miles (0.1 km). Turn right following the signs to El Torcal. Drive on this country road seven miles (11 km). Turn right just after the El Torcal sign and drive uphill two miles (3 km) to reach the parking lot, park information center, and trailhead.

If you are heading out to El Torcal Natural Park after seeing the dolmens, you are going to be detoured through town on some one-way streets. Keep following signs to El Torcal and you should find the road leading out to the park.

To reach Laguna de Fuente de Piedra, exit Antequera towards Jerez and Sevilla. Get on the A-92 towards Sevilla and drive 10 miles (16 km) to the Laguna de Fuente Piedra exit. Loop around and turn right onto the MA-701 and drive over the freeway. In 0.5 miles (0.8 km) go straight at the intersection and follow signs to the lagoon. In 0.2 miles (0.3 km) turn right, in 0.1 miles (0.1 km) turn left, in 0.3 miles (0.5 km) bear right, in 0.4 miles (0.6 km) turn left, and in 0.3 miles (0.5 km) park in the Visitor's Center parking lot.

Antequera Travel Notes:

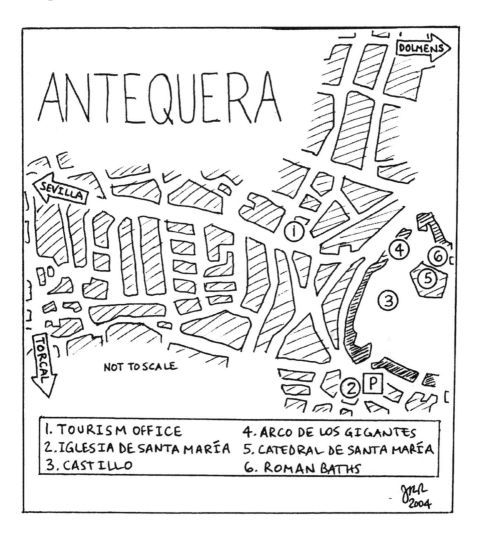

Arcos de la Frontera

Arcos de la Frontera, one of the charming *pueblos blancos* (white villages), is perched on a cliff and filled with white washed houses, narrow and twisting streets, and fabulous old building façades. As a bonus, it's one of the closest *pueblos blancos* to Rota. Arcos is best visited Monday through Saturday in the morning to catch everything open and beat the heat. You can visit the main cathedral, take a walking tour, buy some cookies, eat lunch, and be home before dinner.

Travel time: About 50 minutes.

Things to do in a day:

- ❏ Visit the Tourist Information Office in the plaza across from the Parador to get a map of the city and sign up for a walking tour. The Tourist Office is open on Monday–Saturday from 10:00–15:00 and 16:00–20:30 (15:00–19:30 from October–February).

❏   Linger in the main square, Plaza del Cabildo, and if you don't suffer from acrophobia, look over the balcony to the steep cliffs below. (Allow 15 minutes)

❏   Sip a *café con leche* at the Parador's café while waiting for your walking tour. Enjoy the panoramic views from the terrace outside the bar without paying Parador room rates. (30+ minutes)

❏   Take a walking tour of Arcos. The Old Town Tour starts at 10:30 Monday–Saturday and 17:00 Monday–Friday. The Patios Tour starts at 12:00 Monday–Saturday and 18:30 Monday–Friday. The tours are offered year-round and leave from the plaza outside the Tourist Information Office. 2004 prices: €5 per person. (1–2 hours)

❏   If the tour guide picks the day you visit Arcos to call in sick, grab a map from the Information Office and create your own walking tour. Walk around the church Iglesia de Santa María, wander through narrow cobblestone streets enjoying pots of geraniums suspended on the walls, peek into open patios, and then walk down to the church Iglesia de San Pedro and the nearby lookout Mirador de Abades. (Allow 1–2 hours)

❏   Visit the Iglesia de Santa María after your morning Old Town Tour or before your morning Patios Tour. There is so much to see inside this church, including the body of the third century martyr Saint Felix inside a glass coffin. If you have a sense of the macabre, look closely and see his bones beneath the wire mesh supporting his clothes. Open on Monday–Friday from 10:00–13:00 and 15:30–18:30, and Saturday from 10:00–14:00. (Allow 30 minutes)

❏   Buy cookies from the nuns at the Convento de las Mercedarias Descalzas, located on Calle Escribanos. Step through the doorway and ring the bell if no one is in line in front of you. Ask for cookies (*galletas*), and then some homemade, boxed cookies should rotate out on a lazy Susan. Choose your favorite selection and put your money on the table. It will rotate around to the nuns and return with your change. 2004 prices: €5 for a box of tasty Spanish-style cookies. Open daily from 8:30–14:30 and 17:00–19:00. (Allow five minutes unless you have to stand in a long line)

❑   Shop for some local artwork at San Pedro Galleria de Arte just beyond the Iglesia de San Pedro on the opposite side of the street. Here you will find local artists' paintings, ceramics, and even some of the cotton rugs for which Arcos is known. (Allow 20+ minutes if you like to shop)

Food tips: There are plenty of little restaurants to be found in Arcos. Restaurante Casa Ramón, located past the convent on the other side of the street, is a pleasant, cool stop. We were able to get lunch fairly early (13:00), eat from the *menu del dia* for eight euros, and relax in a dining room filled with pretty mirrors, plates, and tiles for sale.

On the opposite side of the street, just past the open market, is the enclosed Plaza Círculo de la Unión. It's full of flowers in the summer, and when there is no breeze, it's as hot as Hades in the sun. It can make for a nice break when you need a cool drink or, if the time is right for *tapas*, some tasty *chocos fritos* (deep fried cuttlefish that taste like calamari, served with a lemon.)

If your palette is refined and your pockets are deep, Restaurante El Convento (located at Marques Torresoto 7) is reputedly the best restaurant in Arcos. Unfortunately, it was closed when we tried to visit one Saturday afternoon.

Highlight: The views. Panoramic views from the Plaza del Cabildo, the *miradors*, and the terrace of the Parador are incomparable.

Lowlight: Discovering the World Motorbike Championship racecourse is on the way to Arcos on the A-382 and getting stuck in outrageous race traffic during the month of May. If you hear it's race week, go another time!

Sidelight: Heading out in late May or early June? You will enjoy postcard-worthy fields of yellow sunflowers on your drive.

Hint: For those with strollers or not wanting to hike, pay parking is available at the top of the city next to the Parador. Follow signs to "Parador". However, the lot tends to be crowded and there are no guarantees your car's paint job will survive the narrow Arcos streets.

Directions: From Rota, drive towards Jerez on the A-491. At the casino/water park traffic circle take the 2:00 exit towards El Portal (CA-201). In six miles (10 km), when the road comes to a 'T' at a traffic circle, turn right onto the A-381. In one mile (1.6 km), take the A-4 north to Sevilla. In three miles (4.8 km) take the A-382 exit. Turn right towards Arcos de la Frontera. Travel 15 miles (24 km) and turn right onto the C-344. Drive about 0.5 miles (0.8 km) through the residential section and bear right following signs for parking "P". In 0.1 miles (0.1 km) turn left up the hill to reach the underground pay parking lot. The gate at the entrance to the underground parking garage closes fast. Unless the timing has been adjusted, you'll have to ride the clutch and gun it once the arm goes up or you'll miss your chance. We have also used the large, dirt parking lot on the right hand side of the street opposite the underground parking turnout. If you park there, cross the footbridge and climb the 130 steps to the city. After parking, follow street signs to the Parador and city center to reach the main plaza. Walking fast, it takes 15 minutes to go from the underground parking lot to the plaza.

Arcos de la Frontera Travel Notes:

NOT TO SCALE

ARCOS DE LA FRONTERA

Baelo Claudia

While Baelo Claudia might not have been considered a seaside resort of the Roman Empire, it certainly feels that way today. You can find ruins of the city located right on the beach, just off the road running from Cádiz to Tarifa. Discover Roman columns, temples, the theater, and the workingman's part of the city—the fish salting factories. Exploring Baelo Claudia is a fine way to spend a sunny afternoon.

Travel time: About one hour 20 minutes.

Things to do in a day:

- ❑ Visit Baelo Claudia and explore the Roman ruins. Open on Sunday from 10:00–14:00. Open on Tuesday–Saturday from 10:00–20:00 (June–September); 10:00–19:00 (October); 10:00–18:00 (November–February); and 10:00–19:00 (March–May). Closed on Monday and major holidays. You can enter up to 30 minutes prior to the closing time. 2004 prices: €1.50. (Allow one hour to visit)

Food tip: As you exit the ruins there are three waterside cabana-style restaurants that do a brisk business: Restaurante Báhia, Restaurante Otero, and Restaurante Miramar. Local fish is the specialty, reasonable prices and great views are the attraction.

Highlight: A nice day in general—a lovely drive past green fields and grazing bulls, a beautiful seaside setting, and historical Roman ruins—all without spending a fortune.

Lowlight: My rudimentary Spanish. The descriptive signs at the ruins would have been much more enlightening had my Spanish been better.

Sidelight: Leave your car in the parking lot of Baelo Claudia and hit the beach. Take the steps past the restaurants down to the sand. This stretch isn't called the windy coast for nothing. You can expect wind and a little blowing sand, but also a clean beach, fishing boats in the water, windsurfers off the coast, and possibly some healthy looking bulls lounging next to the sand.

Hint: This is a notoriously windy area. Even if it's calm and sunny when you leave the house, expect a stiff breeze when you arrive. Bring a windbreaker.

Directions: From Rota, take the A-491 to the El Paseo mall traffic circle. Take the 3:00 exit on the N-IV towards Algeciras. Follow N-IV traffic signs through several traffic circles. In about 11 miles (18 km) follow the A-48/E-5 towards Algeciras. About 65 miles (105 km) from Rota you will turn right onto the CA-2216. In 0.5 miles (0.8 km) bear right, and in 2.5 miles (four km) turn left. In 0.2 miles (0.3 km) bear right to reach the parking lot straight ahead on your right. Pay the typical dirt parking lot fees.

Baelo Claudia Travel Notes:

Benalup—Casas Viejas

Benalup—Casas Viejas's claim to fame dates back to the Neolithic Age—that's roughly 7,000–10,000 years ago. I looked it up. The main attraction is a cave, the Tajo de las Figuras, that shows a collection of prehistoric drawings ranging from the Neolithic Age to the Age of Metals. The cave itself is pretty small, but its walls are covered in faded ancient art. Quite possibly, this is the oldest manmade thing you'll ever see, so grab a historian and your hiking boots, and make the drive out to Benalup.

Travel time: About one hour 20 minutes.

Things to do in a day:

❏ See the cave, Tajo de las Figuras, and its prehistoric art. From the road, plan to hike uphill on a rocky trail for 20 minutes before reaching the cave. Climb a very steep ladder to a small viewing platform to see inside. Afterwards, follow the guard to a series of exposed tombs carved out of the rocks a short distance away. Open on Wednesday–Sunday from 9:00–15:00, closed Monday and Tuesday. Free. (Allow 1+ hours)

Food tip: The hotel-restaurant Cortijo de las Gruellas is an easy place to stop if you'd like lunch. It's located at the first traffic circle straight ahead as you enter Benalup. They have a pleasant outdoor patio surrounded by balconies and colorful, climbing bougainvillea. We especially enjoyed the gazpacho, which was presented in large wooden bowls with a small plate of chopped veggies and ham to garnish the soup with.

Highlight: Seeing figures firsthand that had been painted *thousands* of years ago.

Lowlight: This was our *second* trip to Benalup to see figures that had been painted *thousands* of years ago. During our first trip, when we arrived at the entrance on the road, the site looked deserted and it had a barbed wire gate that seemed to prevent access. So we wandered around a bit and then left. Come to find out, that's how it looks when it *is* open. One lonely guard sits up at the top near the cave and guides people in when they arrive at the cave entrance. Unfortunately, he's completely hidden from view down at the road. It took a second trip to Benalup, and backtracking to the Information Office, to discover this.

Sidelight: If you just can't seem to visit a city without getting out and exploring a bit, try the Ruta de las Fuentes Urbanas in Benalup. Benalup is an area known for its natural springs, and there are six natural springs located within the city and more located outside the city. Pick up a guide from the Information Office that lists the locations of all the springs and start your exploring. Just be aware that the natural spring waters now come from a faucet into a basin, so it's not bubbling up from the earth before your very eyes.

Hint: Learn from my experience. If you are at the restaurant Cortijo de las Gruellas (or any Spanish restaurant, for that matter) and you feel like having salmon but they're out of it, don't mistake *salmonete* for a close alternative. This red mullet fish comes to you served in its full splendor. While I can make the best of a fish served with its head and tail still attached, to have to watch every forkful because you're afraid of getting a mouth full of fish entrails doesn't make for the most pleasant meal.

Directions: From Rota, drive towards Jerez on the A-491. At the casino/water park traffic circle take the 2:00 exit towards El Portal (CA-201). In six miles (10 km), when the road comes to a 'T' at a traffic circle, turn right onto the A-381. Follow this road 17 miles (27 km) then turn right onto the A-393 towards Medina Sidonia. About 1.5 miles (2.4 km) from the A-381, bypass Medina Sidonia and follow signs pointing towards Benalup on the CA-211 and Vejer de la Frontera on the A-393. You will go through a number of traffic circles, continue following signs to Benalup and Vejer de la Frontera. About 9.5 miles (15 km) after you exited the A-381, there will be a left hand turn to Benalup. Take this turn and follow the road about six miles (10 km) to reach the edge of town. Go straight through the circle leading into town.

To reach the Tourist Information Office, drive about 0.2 miles (0.3 km) into town, turn right, and the Information Office will be on the next corner on the right.

To reach the caves, follow the main road through the heart of Benalup. Stay on this road, bearing left in 0.4 miles (0.6 km), and leave the village in another 0.2 miles (0.3 km). Drive about five miles (eight km) to the cave, following signs to Los Barrios. Stay alert, because just before the entrance there's only one sign for Tajo de las Figuras. The entrance off the road is limited to a gated dirt driveway capable of parking one car. If this is already taken, travel back down the road in the direction you came from to the Recreation Area El Celemin on the opposite side of the road next to the reservoir. You can find parking just off the road here, and then walk back 0.5 miles (0.8 km) to the entrance and trailhead to the cave.

Once at the entrance, you've got some hiking ahead of you. As long as you are within the visiting hours, climb through the barbed wire gate (the one that makes the site looks like it's closed to the public) and start your hike. Walk to the right, passing the deserted-looking "ticket booth", and follow the rocky trail uphill. Turn right near the top of the hill following small signs to the cave. Shortly, you'll reach the bottom of a steep ladder leading to the cave. A guard will unlock the ladder for you, guide you up, and afterwards he'll lead you to the open tombs a short distance away.

Benalup—Casas Viejas Travel Notes:

Cádiz I

Cádiz was founded by the Phoenicians and is considered to be the oldest city in Europe. While not much is left from the Phoenicians other than two impressive Phoenician sarcophagi displayed in the Museo de Cádiz, you should see the city and its other highlights just for the bragging rights of visiting Europe's oldest city.

Travel time: About 35 minutes on the train from the El Puerto de Santa María train station to Cádiz. See Cádiz II for information on taking the ferry from El Puerto de Santa María to Cádiz.

Things to do in a day:

- ❑ Visit the Plaza de España, a monument to the signing of the 1812 Constitution. (Allow 15 minutes)

- ❑ Walk the "red line" route through the old city. It begins near the Plaza de España and ends near the train station. (Allow one hour to stroll the route)

- ❑ Visit the Museo de Cádiz on the Plaza de Mina as you walk through the historic city. Check out an eclectic collection of Phoenician sarcophagi, Roman coins, and fine arts. Museum descriptions are in Spanish only. Open Tuesday from 14:30–2000; Wednesday–Saturday from 9:00–20:00; and Sunday from 9:30–14:30. 2003 prices: €1.50. (Allow one hour)

- ❑ Detour off the red line for some shopping on the pedestrian street, Ancha. Some Cádiz shops feature amber jewelry harkening back to the days when the Phoenicians used to trade amber as a commodity. (Allow 30 minutes)

- ❑ See the beautiful 18th century architecture of the golden-domed New Cathedral.

Food tip: If you are following the red line, look for one of Cádiz's many bakeries between the Plaza de Mina and the Plaza de las Flores. Go in and take a peek! Experience one of the joys of traveling—a delicacy from a local baker.

Highlight: After numerous trips to the city, we were *finally* able to visit the Museo de Cádiz and see the Phoenician sarcophagi. Check the museum's opening times before you go.

Lowlight: One unhappy train conductor. Not realizing we had purchased a ticket for the slower regional train, we hopped on the Andalucían Express, the first train at the station. The train conductor was clearly displeased. After shaking his head in disgust, he ignored us for the rest of the voyage. Not knowing what we did wrong, we spent the next 25 minutes fervently hoping the train would end up in Cádiz. It did.

Sidelight: For a unique travel experience, take the ferry over from El Puerto de Santa María. See Cádiz II for directions.

Hint: It's very helpful to have a map of the city before you set out on your walk. There may be many streets going through repair and the red line may be torn up along with the sidewalk. If you don't have a map, take one of the bus pamphlets that tour guides are always trying to hand you. It has a nice map of the city and should include the red line tourist route.

Directions: From the El Puerto de Santa María train station, take the Andalucían Express or the regional train, Cercanias, to Cádiz. Check out www.renfe.es/ingles for timetables and prices. You can drive to Cádiz, but parking is tight and once you get there you will be walking anyway. My advice, take the train.

As you exit the Cádiz train station, you will roughly be facing west. The Bay of Cádiz will be on your right hand side and the old city will be straight ahead and on your left. To begin the "red line" tourist walk through the historical city, head to the Plaza de España. To get there, start walking with the bay on your right hand side, on the opposite side of the street from the harbor. First pass the Plaza de Sevilla (with a fountain), walk through the gardens of Paseo de Canalejas, bear slightly to your right, and straight ahead will be the Plaza de España (about a 10 minute walk from the train station). The "red line" route begins here at the Plaza de España. Look for the painted red line on the sidewalk.

Cádiz Travel Notes:

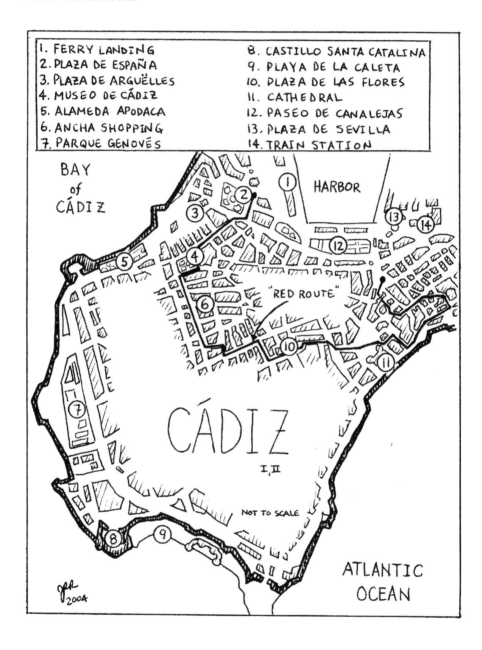

1. FERRY LANDING
2. PLAZA DE ESPAÑA
3. PLAZA DE ARGUËLLES
4. MUSEO DE CÁDIZ
5. ALAMEDA APODACA
6. ANCHA SHOPPING
7. PARQUE GENOVÉS
8. CASTILLO SANTA CATALINA
9. PLAYA DE LA CALETA
10. PLAZA DE LAS FLORES
11. CATHEDRAL
12. PASEO DE CANALEJAS
13. PLAZA DE SEVILLA
14. TRAIN STATION

BAY of CÁDIZ

HARBOR

"RED ROUTE"

CÁDIZ

I, II

NOT TO SCALE

ATLANTIC OCEAN

Cádiz II

Not only is Cádiz a great city to explore, it's also a great city to spend more than one carefree day. Cádiz is close enough so you can go to just hang out and not feel guilty if you don't see every tourist spot within a five-mile radius. So pack your picnic and get ready to relax. (Did you get a picnic-in-a-backpack as a wedding gift? This is the *perfect* time to use it!) Take the ferry over from El Puerto de Santa María for a change of pace.

Travel time: Approximately one hour. About 15 minutes to drive to downtown El Puerto de Santa María and 45 minutes on the ferry to the Cádiz Maritime Station.

Things to do in a day:

- ❑ Kick back on the ferry, El Vaporcito, for a ride across the Bay of Cádiz. 2003 schedule: departs Puerto at 9:00, 11:00, 13:00, 15:30, 17:30, (and 19:30 in the summer), departs Cádiz at 10:00, 12:00, 14:00, 16:30, 18:30, (and 20:30 in the summer). Closed Monday in the winter. 2003 prices: €4.50 roundtrip. (45 minutes)

- ❑ Walk along the Atlantic Ocean and through the park, Alameda Apodaca.

- ❑ Picnic on a grassy area in the Parque Genovés. Look for squawking parrots in the palm trees.

- ❑ Visit the 16th-17th century Castillo Santa Catalina and the museum inside. Special art exhibits are displayed. Open daily from 10:00–13:30 and 17:00–18:30. Free.

- ❑ Dip your feet (or more) into the Atlantic at the beach Playa de la Caleta.

Food tip: The ferry has reasonably priced refreshments to purchase on the lower-deck level. You may find chips and a cold beverage a fine way to end a relaxing day in the sun.

Highlight: A day of rest—unusual in our hectic lifestyle chasing after a toddler.

Lowlight: Hustling back from the beach to catch the ferry after a leisurely day of play. Be aware it takes about 40 minutes at a quick walk to go from the end of the Playa de la Caleta to board the boat if you make a quick stop to purchase an ice cream along the way.

Sidelight: James Bond fans take note: the beach in Cádiz, Playa de la Caleta, is the beach used in the scene where Hale Berry emerges from the water in *Die Another Day*. In the film you can see the fortress island beyond the beach, and you may recognize other parts of Cádiz used to portray Havana, Cuba in the movie.

Hint: On the lower level of the ferry at the stern, there's a spot for a few people to sit, kick their legs out, and catch some rays while making the bay crossing.

Directions: First, pack your picnic. This is a great picnic day.

Leaving Naval Base Rota by the Puerto gate, turn left on the CA-603 to head to El Puerto de Santa María. You will go through a number of traffic circles. At the traffic circle about 5.0 miles (eight km) from Naval Base Rota, take the 11:00 exit following signs to "centro ciudad". Get in the right lane and bear right in 0.2 miles (0.3 km). In 0.1 miles (0.1 km) take the 1:00 exit at the traffic circle. Drive about 0.7 miles (1.1 km) passing the bullring and *bodega* (winery) warehouses. At the 'T' intersection turn left and drive parallel to the river for about 0.4 miles (0.6 km). There is a cobblestone pay parking lot at the bend in the road to the right.

Catch the ferry just outside the parking lot entrance—look for the large, black, iron gates. A small ferry sign with the schedule should be posted on the gate, or a schedule can be obtained from the Tourist Information Office located a few blocks up from the ferry landing on Calle Luna. Call 629-46-8014 for more information. Purchase your tickets onboard once you set sail.

When you reach Cádiz, exit the Maritime Station, cross the street, turn to the left, and head to the Plaza de España by bearing right onto Avenida de América. Once in the plaza, turn to the right and head to the Atlantic via Plaza de

Argüelles. Follow the coastline and keep the Atlantic on your right to reach the gardens and the beach.

Cádiz Travel Notes:

Carmona

Carmona has a little something for everyone. Pick your favorite among churches, convents, bell towers, family mansions, Roman cemeteries, and defensive city gates. Walk Carmona's cobblestone streets and step into history.

Travel time: Approximately one hour 30 minutes.

Things to do in a day:

❏ Visit the Roman Necropolis where you can climb down a ladder into a dark 2000-year old crypt. The guided tour is in Spanish but there are signs with descriptions in English. Tours leave every 30 minutes Tuesday–Friday and every 45 minutes Saturday–Sunday. There is a museum to bide your time while waiting for your tour. Hours from September 16–June 14 are Tuesday–Friday from 9:00–17:00 and

Saturday–Sunday from 10:00–14:00. Closed Monday and holidays. Hours from June 15–September 15 are Tuesday–Friday from 8:30–14:00 and Saturday from 10:00–14:00. Closed Sunday, Monday, and holidays. Located at Avenida de Jorge Bonsor 9. Free. (1+ hours for the tour and museum)

❑ Hike through the town to see historical buildings, churches, the Puerta de Sevilla, and the Puerta de Córdoba. It is helpful to have a city map, but if one is not available, follow signs to the historical center and wander around. (Allow 1–2 hours)

❑ Visit the Parador (state-run hotel) located at the top of the hill with a lovely central courtyard and splendid vistas of the countryside. (Allow 30 minutes)

Food tip: Visit the bar at the Parador for a *café con leche* or the restaurant for an excellent lunch. You can enjoy the breathtaking views without paying breathtaking prices for an overnight stay. The menu of the day was about 20 euros per person including dessert, while an overnight stay in 2003 ran about 120 euros. Current room rates can be found at www.parador.es.

Highlight: Unparalleled views of the countryside while enjoying a fine lunch at the Parador.

Lowlight: Knowing that we weren't staying at the aforementioned Parador that night…sigh.

Sidelight: The Carmona Parador is a modern building built on the grounds of Pedro the Cruel's palace. Who was Pedro the Cruel? Read about him and brush up on your Spanish medieval history on the web. Stanley G. Payne wrote *A History of Spain and Portugal* that can be found at http://libro.uca.edu.payne1/.

In short, Pedro the Cruel succeeded his father Alfonso XI as king at the age of sixteen in 1350. He earned the nickname "the Cruel" from his enemies—one of whom was his half-brother, Enrique. Pedro had his late father's mistress, Leonor de Guzmán, put to death. Because of this, her adult son, Enrique, revolted against the crown. Enrique and his followers stuck Pedro with the name "Pedro the Cruel" and gained support from France and Aragón in what became the Great Castilian Civil War.

Under Edward the Black Prince, the English supported Pedro for a time, but after falling out over money issues they pulled their support, giving Enrique's forces the eventual victory. Enrique (the Not-So-Nice-Himself) personally killed Pedro, executed royalist leaders, and—despite his illegitimacy—reigned as King Enrique II from 1369–1379.

Hint: If you don't want to hike the hill to the Parador you can drive and park in the Parador's small parking area.

Directions: From Rota, drive towards Jerez on the A-491. At the casino/water park traffic circle take the 2:00 exit towards El Portal (CA-201). In six miles (10 km), when the road comes to a 'T' at a traffic circle, turn right onto the A-381. In one mile (1.6 km), take the A-4 north to Sevilla for approximately 50 miles (80 km). Turn right onto the N-IV/E-5 to Córdoba, which is also the way to the Sevilla airport. About 21 miles (34 km) after you turn onto the N-IV/E-5, take the Carmona exit. In about two miles (three km) you will reach a traffic circle with a statue of a Roman lady. Take the 9:00 exit and follow the signs pointing to the Roman Necropolis. In 0.1 miles (0.1 km) turn left at the intersection and drive 0.1 miles (0.1 km) to the entrance of the necropolis on the left. The necropolis is located behind a tall wall and the Roman Amphitheater can be seen on your right. The sign near the entrance reads "Conjunto Arqueológico de Carmona". Park on the street.

To reach the historic center of Carmona, head back to the circle with the Roman Lady Statue and take the 9:00 exit, continuing in the direction you were heading coming into town. Follow signs toward the Parador and historical center. In less than 0.5 miles (0.8 km) you will reach a large plaza that has pay underground parking. Park here and walk to explore the old city.

Continue to follow signs to the historic center and you will reach the Puerta de Sevilla. Large and imposing, you can't miss it. There is a Tourist Information Office located within the double gate where you can get a city map to explore further.

Carmona Travel Notes:

1. ROMAN NECROPOLIS
2. ROMAN AMPHITHEATER
3. PUERTA DE SEVILLA
4. TOURISM OFFICE
5. PARADOR
6. PUERTA DE CÓRDOBA

Chipiona

If you like relaxing days, beach towns, and interesting architecture, visit Chipiona. Since it's just up the road from Rota, you might be tempted to think it's just more of the same local flavor. Don't be misled—Chipiona has its own unique personality. If you visit in the off-season (September through June), the beaches are empty and the parking is free, but unfortunately none of the ice cream stands are open. If you visit in August, the peak of the tourist season, be prepared for huge crowds of Europeans enjoying their summer holiday. The entire beach path is paved, so this makes a good day trip if you travel with a stroller.

Travel time: About 20 minutes.

Things to do in a day:

❑ Hit the beach for an hour or two. The beach next to the port, Playa Cruz del Mar, is a wide sandy stretch on the Atlantic. Feel the sand

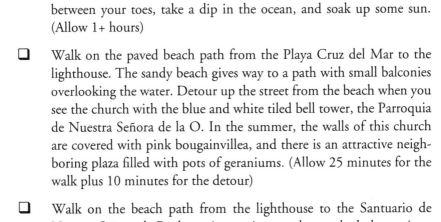

between your toes, take a dip in the ocean, and soak up some sun. (Allow 1+ hours)

❏ Walk on the paved beach path from the Playa Cruz del Mar to the lighthouse. The sandy beach gives way to a path with small balconies overlooking the water. Detour up the street from the beach when you see the church with the blue and white tiled bell tower, the Parroquia de Nuestra Señora de la O. In the summer, the walls of this church are covered with pink bougainvillea, and there is an attractive neighboring plaza filled with pots of geraniums. (Allow 25 minutes for the walk plus 10 minutes for the detour)

❏ Walk on the beach path from the lighthouse to the Santuario de Nuestra Señora de Regla, an interesting, modern cathedral on prime, beach front property. (Allow 20 minutes)

❏ Turn around and walk back from the cathedral, past the lighthouse, to the Playa Cruz del Mar and your car. (Allow 45 minutes)

Food tip: If you didn't bring a picnic for the beach, there are plenty of food options. Lining the beach path there are a multitude of cafes and restaurants advertising seafood and paella as their specialties. From the southern end of Playa Cruz del Mar to the lighthouse there are small cafes with local atmosphere. Between the lighthouse and cathedral, the cafés tend to cater to the vacationing beach crowds.

Highlight: A stress-free afternoon spent on the beach, followed by a pleasant walk through town.

Lowlight: Too many aging, European men in Speedos.

Sidelight: There is a great family-oriented park located on the way to Chipiona in Costa Ballena. At the park there are acres of grass to run on, playground equipment, walking paths, and a large pond with ducks and geese to feed. (Remember to bring stale bread, and watch your fingers with the geese!) I wouldn't necessarily add this side trip onto your beach day, but if you want an enjoyable way to spend a summer evening with the kids, try this park.

Hint: If you spend any amount of time at the beach, bring a beach umbrella for that strong Spanish sun.

Directions: From Naval Base Rota, exit the Rota gate and take an immediate right onto the CA-603. Drive three miles (five km) and get onto the A-491 towards Chipiona. Drive approximately six miles (10 km) to Chipiona. At the traffic circle, take the 9:00 exit onto Avenida de Rota. Drive towards the city center, go straight through the traffic circle at 0.4 miles (0.6 km), and turn right onto Avenida de la Disputacion at 0.9 miles (1.5 km). There will be a gas station on the opposite right hand corner where you turn. Drive on Avenida de la Disputacion about 0.2 miles (0.3 km) and at the traffic "square" take the 9:00 exit onto Avenida Rocio Jurado. Drive about 0.2 miles (0.3 km) to reach a traffic circle with a fountain and a large sculpture of a woman, the Monumento a Rocio Jurado. Take the 10:00 exit. The port will be on your right and the beach straight ahead. There is ample parking along this street. On the Chipiona city map it looks like a bypass road is in the works. When this opens up, the directions will likely change.

To get to the Costa Ballena park, exit the Naval Base by the Rota gate, turn right, drive three miles (five km), and get onto the A-491 towards Chipiona. Drive about 3.2 miles (five km) and turn left. This is the second Costa Ballena exit. Drive about 0.2 miles (0.3 km) and there will be a large park on your right hand side just before you reach Gran Hotel Colon. Look behind the large hibiscus bushes bordering the road to see the park.

Chipiona Travel Notes:

1. MARINA
2. MONUMENTO A ROCIO JURADO
3. PLAYA CRUZ DEL MAR
4. PARROQUIA DE NUESTRA SEÑORA DE LA O
5. PLAZA DEL CASTILLO
6. PLAZA DE LAS AMÉRICAS LIGHTHOUSE
7. SANTUARIO DE NUESTRA SEÑORA DE REGLA

DRIVING ROUTE

ROTA

CHIPIONA

NOT TO SCALE

ATLANTIC OCEAN

2004

Córdoba I

Córdoba is a picturesque city of arches and fountains. It served as the capital of Islamic Spain during the Moorish occupation. Explore Córdoba's Moorish roots, wind your way through the narrow streets of the Jewish Quarter, and experience the unique flavor of this city. While you can see the major sites in a day, there are Moorish ruins outside the city and museums within that warrant a second day in Córdoba. Grab a hotel room, read Córdoba II, and experience a night in this exotic city.

Travel time: About two hours 30 minutes.

Things to do in a day:

- ❑ Walk along the Río Guadalquivir (Guadalquivir River) and cross the Puente Romano (Roman Bridge) for great views of the city. It's called the Roman Bridge, but only the foundations are original Roman.

- ❑ Visit La Mezquita (the mosque-now-cathedral) to see the most renowned part of the city. Wind your way through the hundreds of beautiful columns and arches inside the former mosque. Buy your tickets inside the walled complex in the Plaza de los Naranjos (Orange Tree Patio). Open October–March on Monday–Saturday from 10:00–18:00, and Sunday from 15:30–17:30. Open April–September on Monday–Saturday from 10:00–19:00, and Sunday from 15:30–19:00. 2003 prices: €6. (Allow one hour)

- ❑ Walk up the tiny but popular Calleja de las Flores street for a peek at the tower of La Mezquita framed by hanging pots of flowers.

- ❑ Stroll through the palace and impressive gardens of the Alcázar de los Reyes Cristianos (Palace of the Christian Kings). The formal gardens and network of fountains are some of the best in southern Spain. Open October–April on Tuesday–Saturday from 10:00–14:00 and 16:30–18:30. Open May, June, and September on Tuesday–Saturday from 10:00–14:00 and 17:30–19:30. Open July and August on Tuesday–Saturday from 8:30–14:30 and 20:00–24:00. Open Sunday and holidays from 9:30–14:30. 2003 prices: €2. (Allow 1+ hours)

- ❑ Explore the narrow streets and shops of the Jewish Quarter. Silver filigree jewelry is one specialty of the area. On Calle Judíos look for "Zoco", a small patio enclosed by workshops of local craftsmen.

- ❑ Visit the 700-year old synagogue on Calle Judíos. It's a small building with only two rooms open to view, but is unique in that it's the only medieval synagogue left in Andalucía. Open on Tuesday–Saturday from 9:30–14:00 and 15:30–17:30, and Sunday from 9:30–14:00. Nominal entrance fee charged. (Allow 15 minutes)

Food tips: There are numerous cafés around La Mezquita and the surrounding area, including Oh La La, the popular restaurant located in the Jewish Quarter. If you like gazpacho, you may want to try the *salmorejo*. This thick Córdoban version of the Andalucían specialty is more like a meal than a soup.

Highlight: Visiting La Mezquita and experiencing the atmosphere created by the hundreds of narrow Moorish columns and arches.

Lowlight: Negotiating the city streets trying to find our hotel with vague verbal directions and erratically placed hotel signs.

Sidelight: If you have the opportunity, visit Córdoba in early May when the Patio Festival is celebrated. The city's residents throw open their doors and show-case their colorful patios. Check the Tourist Information Office for walking routes.

Hint: You might be tempted to park on the street on the other side of the river and walk across the Roman Bridge since the parking here is free. Don't do it. We saw some very unhappy German tourists with a shattered car window who wished they had parked in a more secure location.

Directions: From Rota, drive towards Jerez on the A-491. At the casino/water park traffic circle take the 2:00 exit towards El Portal (CA-201). In six miles (10 km), when the road comes to a 'T' at a traffic circle, turn right onto the A-381. In one mile (1.6 km), take the A-4 north to Sevilla for approximately 50 miles (80 km). Turn right onto the N-IV/E-5 to Córdoba, which is also the way to the Sevilla airport. Travel about 92 miles (148 km) on the N-IV/E-5 and take a left-hand exit to Córdoba. Follow signs to *centro ciudad*, the city center. For easy parking, drive on the main road about two miles (3.2 km) from the N-IV/E-5 and cross the Río Guadalquivir on the San Rafael Bridge. There will be old Moorish walls to your right. Two-tenths of a mile (0.3 km) past the river there is a stoplight. Turn right at the light and take an immediate right to find a pay dirt parking lot next to the Moorish walls.

If you are without a map, first head towards the Tourist Information Office on the west side of La Mezquita. Out of the parking lot, follow the sidewalk back down to the river on the road you came in on, and turn left at the river. Follow this road until you reach the next bridge, El Puente Romano. Turn left, and an old arched city gate (La Puerta del Punte) and La Mezquita will be in front of you. Circle the walls of La Mezquita to the left and you will find the Tourist Information Office on your left.

Córdoba is also accessible by train, but most trains running between Sevilla and Córdoba are the pricey AVE trains. Check out www.renfe.es/ingles for time-tables and prices.

Córdoba Travel Notes:

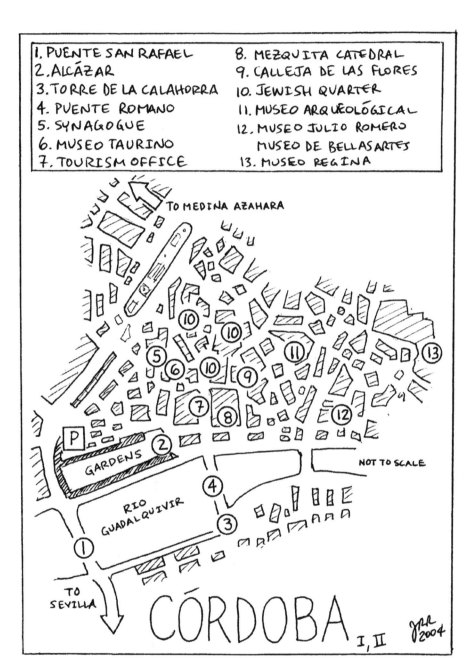

1. PUENTE SAN RAFAEL
2. ALCÁZAR
3. TORRE DE LA CALAHORRA
4. PUENTE ROMANO
5. SYNAGOGUE
6. MUSEO TAURINO
7. TOURISM OFFICE
8. MEZQUITA CATEDRAL
9. CALLEJA DE LAS FLORES
10. JEWISH QUARTER
11. MUSEO ARQUEOLÓGICAL
12. MUSEO JULIO ROMERO
    MUSEO DE BELLAS ARTES
13. MUSEO REGINA

TO MEDINA AZAHARA

P
GARDENS
NOT TO SCALE
RIO GUADALQUIVIR
TO SEVILLA
CÓRDOBA I, II
2004

Córdoba II

If you love the atmosphere of Córdoba, spend a second day here exploring the area's Moorish roots and soaking up some local colors and flavors of this beautiful city. If you are impressed with archeological ruins (and who isn't?), Medina Azahara is worth the trip alone.

Travel time: About two hours 30 minutes to arrive in Córdoba, plus 15 minutes to Medina Azahara outside of town.

Things to do in a day:

❏ Hike around Medina Azahara, a large but short-lived Moorish city over 1000 years old. See tumbled down ruins and painstakingly restored arches, columns, and decorative walls. Open May 1–September 15 on Tuesday–Saturday from 10:00–20:30, and Sunday and holidays from 10:00–14:00. Open September 16–April 30 on Tuesday–Sunday from 10:00–14:00. Closed Monday and enough other days to take particular notice: January 1, January 6, February 28, Good Friday, May 1, August 15, October 24, November 1, December 24, December 25, and December 31. 2003 prices: €1.50. (Allow 1.5 hours)

❏ Back in Córdoba, visit your choice of museums:

• The Museo Arqueológico (Archeology Museum). See Roman sarcophagi, statues and mosaics, and a fine bronze stag that survived the plundering of Medina Azahara. Open on Tuesday from 15:00–20:00; Wednesday–Saturday from 9:00–20:00; and Sunday from 9:00–15:00. Closed Monday. Located at Plaza de Jerónimo Páez 7. 2003 prices: €1.50. (Allow 30+ minutes)

• The Museo Julio Romero de Torres. Dedicated to this popular Córdoban artist, the museum features numerous paintings of

semi-clad women with passionate eyes. Open October 16–
April 30 on Tuesday–Saturday from 10:00–14:00 and 16:30–
18:30. Open May, June, September, and October 1–15 on
Tuesday–Saturday from 10:00–14:00 and 17:30–19:30. Open
July and August on Tuesday–Saturday from 8:30–14:30. Open
Sunday from 9:30–14:30. Closed Monday. Located at Plaza
del Postro 1. 2003 prices: approximately €3. (Allow 30+ min-
utes)

• The Museo de Bellas Artes (Museum of Fine Arts). See artwork
from the Medieval, Baroque, and Modern eras including a
pleasing kitchen still life with oranges (*Bódegon con Naranjas*)
by Rafael Romero Barros. Open on Tuesday from 15:00–
20:00; Wednesday–Saturday from 9:00–20:00; and Sunday
from 9:00–15:00. Closed Monday. Located across the courtyard from the Museo Julio Romero de Torres at Plaza del Postro 1. 2003 prices: €1.50. (Allow 30+ minutes)

Food tips: If you need a meal after visiting Medina Azahara, try Restaurante Los
Almendros. You may even receive a brochure for it when you park at Medina
Azahara. To get to the restaurant from the Medina, take your first left after leaving the parking lot, and then the next left. Travel two miles (three km) up the
hill, turn left at the intersection and drive 0.5 miles (0.8 km) to the restaurant on
your left. You will pay restaurant prices (read: a little high if you are used to *venta*
prices) but the beer is cold and the *churrasco* (grilled steak) is tasty.

The restaurant El Caballo Rojo is often mentioned as one of the best restaurants in Córdoba. Being on a military budget, I couldn't say…but if you want
some fine pita bread sandwiches, try Olé Kebob located at Calle de Herreria 53
on the road running between La Mezquita and the Museo de Bellas Artes.

Highlight: Discovering Old Córdoba (Medina Azahara) off the beaten track,
nestled in the foothills.

Lowlight: Discovering that those who write tourist books obviously don't travel
in August. Nearly every museum we attempted to tour was closed in the afternoon despite guidebook listings to the contrary. My guess is that July afternoons
are questionable as well.

Sidelight: There are so many museums to visit in Córdoba. If you'd rather, try the Museo Taurino (bullfighting museum), the Museo Regina (jewelry museum), or the Torre de la Calahorra located in the tower across the river. The tower has convenient hours for tourists, but except for a nice rooftop view of La Mezquita, it wasn't worth my four euros. Try it if your kids like dioramas and talking life-size figures won't give them nightmares. Open October–April from 10:00–18:00. Open May–September from 10:00–14:00 and 16:30–20:30.

Hint: Medina Azahara can be hot in the summer and food and drinks are not allowed on the grounds. Conveniently, a truck selling ice cream and cold water is normally located in the parking lot for when you are done.

Directions: From Rota, drive towards Jerez on the A-491. At the casino/water park traffic circle take the 2:00 exit towards El Portal (CA-201). In six miles (10 km), when the road comes to a 'T' at a traffic circle, turn right onto the A-381. In one mile (1.6 km), take the A-4 north to Sevilla for approximately 50 miles (80 km). Turn right onto the N-IV/E-5 to Córdoba, this is also the way to the Sevilla airport. Travel about 92 miles (148 km) on the N-IV/E-5 and take a left-hand exit to Córdoba. Follow signs to the city center, "centro ciudad".

The Medina Azahara (or Medinat Al-Zara on the Spanish signs) is located outside Córdoba off of the A-431 (Ctra. de Palma Río, Km 8). Follow signs to the city center and cross the Río Guadalquivir on the San Rafael Bridge. In 0.6 miles (0.9 km) bear right onto a giant traffic circle. In about 0.3 miles (0.5 km) make a broad left-handed U-turn and in 0.2 miles (0.3 km) turn right onto Avenida de Medina Azahara. Look for signs that point to Medinat Al-Zara and the A-431. It's about 3.5 miles (5.6 km) until you reach a right hand turn to get to the Medina Azahara. Follow the road about 1.3 miles (two km) and bear left to reach a small pay parking lot at the end of the road. As you approach Medina Azahara you may see other cars parked along the road, carefully balanced on the edge of a gully. There's no need to join them, parking in the paved lot is cheap.

One provincial map I have indicates a bypass road to Medina Azahara is being built to avoid driving through the heart of Córdoba. When this is completed, ignore these directions and take the direct route.

For easy city parking back in Córdoba, retrace your steps and use the dirt parking lot mentioned in Córdoba I. Drive on the main road about two miles (three km) from the N-IV/E-5 and cross the Río Guadalquivir on the San Rafael Bridge. There will be old Moorish walls to your right. Two-tenths of a mile (0.3

km) past the river there is a stoplight. Turn right at the light and take an immediate right to find a pay dirt parking lot next to the Moorish walls.

Córdoba Travel Notes:

Doña Blanca

Doña Blanca is an active archeological site that dates back an amazing 2800 years. It was at one point occupied by the Phoenicians and there's lots of information provided about this ancient culture at the site. All the signs are in Spanish, but with some basic language skills you can still glean some interesting facts from them.

Doña Blanca's landmark is the Tower of Doña Blanca, located at the top of the hill. Interesting popular folklore claims the medieval tower to be the place where King Pedro I (also known as Pedro the Cruel) imprisoned his wife, Doña Blanca de Borbón. This landmark is a fascinating piece of history to visit so close to home.

Travel time: About 15 minutes.

Things to do in a day:

- ❑   Visit the archeological ruins. See ancient stone walls, a medieval tower, and active dig sites. Open on Wednesday–Sunday from 11:00–14:00. Closed on Monday, Tuesday, and holidays. Free. (Allow one hour)

Food tip: From Doña Blanca, continue on the CA-201 to El Portal. In 1.8 miles (three km) from Doña Blanca on the left side is Venta El Pollo. There is a large dirt parking lot adjacent to the restaurant. We figured it must be good since every time we drove past, the parking lot was full. We figured right. The food was tasty and the price was right. The grilled chicken (*pollo a la plancha*) was cooked perfectly and the cold, marinated green beans were delicious.

Highlight: Pretty views from the top of Doña Blanca's hill overlooking the neighboring village, the rustling of trees next to a small stream, and standing in the midst of incredibly old ruins.

Lowlight: Due to the neighboring farms, it occasionally smelled like cows.

Sidelight: Since you are visiting local Phoenician ruins, you should know a little about these remarkable people. William McGrath writes up a short history about the Phoenicians in Spain that can be found at www.tuspain.com. Click on the "heritage" link to find his article.

The ancient Phoenicians lived in modern day Lebanon, and flourished from about 1200 BC until 332 BC when Alexander the Great defeated the powerful Phoenician city of Tyre. They were skilled sailors, clever merchants, and excellent craftsmen. They were known for their navigation skills, their purple-dyed textiles (using a rare dye extracted from the Murex snail), and their 22-letter alphabet.

The Phoenician society was based on powerful city-states and they established themselves throughout the Mediterranean, including southern Spain. They found Spain abundant with raw materials such as silver, gold, and copper. While the great Phoenician cities eventually declined, their greatest achievement remains, the beginnings of the modern alphabet.

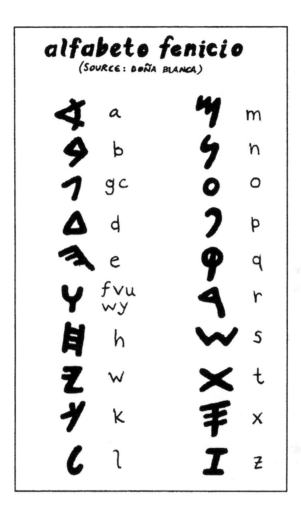

Hints:

1. Don't miss walking into the tower or into the adjacent building that protects a deep dig site.

2. Be cautious of possible beehives in the tower's window.

Directions: From Rota, drive towards Jerez on the A-491. At the casino/water park traffic circle take the 2:00 exit towards El Portal (CA-201). In two miles (three km) on the right hand side is the archeology site. Don't make the right hand turn to the small town Poblado de Doña Blanca. The archeology site is just beyond that intersection on the main road (CA-201). A sign reads, "Yacimiento Arqueológico Doña Blanca". Park to the right of the entrance.

Doña Blanca Travel Notes:

Doñana National Park

Doñana National Park is one of Spain's natural treasures and it's protected accordingly. To preserve this natural beauty, visitors are only permitted to enter the park on a guided tour—but don't let that stop you. One of the easiest ways to access the park is by boat from Sanlúcar de Barrameda. The boat tour takes you up the Guadalquivir River for a shoreline view of the park and stops several times to enjoy the marshes, woodlands, and meadows. Even if you don't see the elusive Iberian lynx, Doñana is a "must see" on every natural historian's list.

Travel time: About 35 minutes to get to the ferry landing.

Things to do in a day:

- [ ] Visit the Fábrica de Hielo (Ice Factory), a historic building that also serves as the visitor center for Doñana National Park. Pick up your tickets for your boat tour here. Tour the first floor, which covers the park's ecosystems. Explore the second floor that covers the human history associated with the park. Open daily from 9:00–19:00. Free. (Allow 30+ minutes)

❑   Hop on the double-decker boat, Real Fernando, at the pier across the street. Spend the next 3.0–3.5 hours discovering Doñana. Tours run November–February at 10:00; March–May and October at 10:00 and 16:00; and June–September at 10:00 and 17:00. Call 956-36-3813 in advance to make your reservation. 2004 prices: €14.64. Note: sometimes the following itinerary is run in reverse.

- Travel about 30 minutes up the river and watch for hawks, herons, and flamingos.

- Spend one hour at the first stop, Pobledo de la Plancha, to see some examples of huts built using Doñana's natural resources and to take a short hike through the umbrella pines to the observation areas in the woodland clearings. Look for red deer, fallow deer, wild boar, Andalucían cows, and the unlikely-to-be-seen Iberian lynx.

- Travel 30 minutes to the second stop, Las Salinas, and disembark in Doñana *Natural* Park. Spend 30 minutes viewing the marshes and birds.

- Travel one hour back to Sanlúcar while watching a movie presentation about Doñana in Spanish.

Food tips: If you're hungry on the boat you're in luck. On the second level there's a little bar that sells snacks and drinks. Need a meal after your trip? If you can afford it, eat at one of the restaurants at Bajo de Guía. The restaurants are located right on the waterfront next to the Fábrica de Hielo. These restaurants offer delicious food and outdoor dining with views of the river and Doñana behind. The seafood is excellent—the chefs there can make even the scary-looking anglerfish taste good—but don't expect to find any bargains.

Highlight: Taking the tour in spring (bird migration season), we were able to spot a black kite, gray heron, imperial eagles, numerous flamingos, shorebirds, and black-winged stilts.

Lowlight: Spring is also rainy season and we endured sheeting rain every time we stepped off the boat.

Sidelight: If the weather is nice and you fancy a stroll, walk back towards the center of town via Avenida Bajo de Guía to check out the residential area. The houses here are more like mansions, with impressive gardens, stained glass windows, and enviable square footage.

Hints:

1. Go to www.visitasdonana.com for more information about the boat tour.

2. Visit www.donana.es and click on Turismo de Doñana for information on the birds and wildlife found in the park.

3. If you forgot to bring your binoculars, rent them onboard. You get close to wildlife, but not *that* close.

Directions: From Naval Base Rota, exit the Rota gate and take an immediate right onto the CA-603. Drive three miles (five km) and get onto the A-491 towards Chipiona. Drive approximately three miles (five km) and turn right following signs to Sanlúcar de Barrameda. Drive six miles (10 km) and turn right at the stop sign. Drive one mile (1.6 km) to reach a large traffic circle with a McDonalds. Take the 9:00 exit towards the beaches. Travel about 0.8 miles (1.3 km) towards the beaches and turn right at the light onto Avenida Bajo de Guía. Signs point to "Bajo de Guía" and "P.N. Doñana". Drive about 0.7 miles (1.1 km) to reach the Bajo de Guía area. Find a parking area on your left, or make a right at the last intersecting street to reach a pay parking lot on your immediate left. Your first stop, the Fábrica de Hielo is further down the road on your right (Bajo de Guía, s/n).

From El Puerto de Santa María, it is quicker to go to Sanlúcar via the CA-602. Take the A-491 to the El Puerto/Sanlúcar exit and turn left onto the CA-602. Follow this road 12 miles (19 km) and you will enter Sanlúcar. At the traffic light, turn left, following signs to the beaches and city center. In about 0.7 miles (1.1 km) at the large traffic circle with the McDonalds take the 3:00 exit towards the beaches. Travel about 0.8 miles (1.3 km) towards the beaches and turn right at the light onto Avenida Bajo de Guía. Signs point to "Bajo de Guía" and "P.N. Doñana". Drive about 0.7 miles (1.1 km) to reach the Bajo de Guía area. Find a parking area on your left, or make a right at the last intersecting street to reach a pay parking lot on your immediate left. Your first stop, the Fábrica de Hielo is further down the road on your right (Bajo de Guía, s/n).

Doñana National Park Travel Notes:

Doñana Natural Park

This is a day trip for those of you who *really* like hiking, nature, or bird watching. Not one of the above? Turn the page; there are probably better day trips for you. That being said, if you enjoy a hike but haven't found the time or place yet, get off the couch and head to Doñana Natural Park.

Travel time: Approximately 40 minutes. The Natural Park is located northeast of Sanlúcar along the Guadalquivir River and marshlands.

Things to do in a day:

- ❑ Walk a few minutes from the parking area to the duck blind to get a good view of the water birds in the lagoon.

- ❑ Take a hike on some sandy trails. The map near the duck blind shows a five kilometer, two hour circular route, but with crisscrossing trails you'll be lucky to follow the exact route. We hiked 45 minutes out then retraced our steps through the network of narrow, sandy trails.

- ❑ Look for lizard tracks, bird tracks, and rabbit tracks since you're unlikely to actually see any of these animals if hiking in the mid-day summer heat.

Food tip: Travel just a few minutes into the park and turn right to the recreation area of Pinares de La Algaida. You will find a multitude of picnic tables—hope you brought a lunch. If not, you passed a McDonald's on your way from Rota at the large traffic circle with a fountain.

Highlight: Enjoying the sounds of nature while hiking: the wind through the pines, the chirp of the crickets, and the sounds of the birds in the air.

Lowlight: Take your pick: a nightmare drive through Sanlúcar to locate the park entrance, hiking without a real destination, August heat, persistent flies, or a baby who got sunscreen in his eyes.

Sidelight: The map at the park entrance shows a bicycle route through the area. You would assume they mean mountain bikes, but the only bikes we observed were motorized dirt bikes. If you like mountain biking, forget the hike, because biking looks like it would be a lot of fun.

Hints:

1. Wear hiking boots, not sport sandals.

2. The trails are sandy and not suitable for a stroller. No, not even a jogging stroller.

3. Bring your sport utility vehicle if you have it. The paved road in the park has huge potholes.

4. Bring binoculars for the duck blind if you are really into bird watching. Of course, if you are really into bird watching, you probably don't need to be told that!

Directions: From Naval Base Rota, exit the Rota gate and take an immediate right onto the CA-603. Drive three miles (five km) and get onto the A-491 towards Chipiona. Drive approximately three miles (five km) and turn right following signs to Sanlúcar de Barrameda. Drive six miles (10 km) and turn right at the stop sign. Drive one mile (1.6 km) to reach a large traffic circle with a McDonalds, go straight. Follow the road approximately 0.7 miles (1.1 km) until you reach a main intersection with a stoplight and signs pointing to Jerez and Puerto. Turn left at the light. From the light, drive 0.1 miles (0.1 km) and go straight through a traffic circle with a statue, and in 0.4 miles (0.6 km) straight through the next circle. In 0.1 miles (0.1 km) there is a traffic "oval", take the 11:00 exit (not the 1:00 exit). Travel two miles (three km) to come to the end of the road. Turn left and then right at the stop sign at the next street. Stay on this main road, and in about 3.8 miles (six km) you will reach the park entrance. There will be a dirt parking area to your left.

From El Puerto de Santa María, it is quicker to go to Sanlúcar via the CA-602. Take the A-491 to the El Puerto/Sanlúcar exit and turn left onto the CA-602. Follow this road 12 miles (19 km) and you will enter Sanlúcar. At the traffic light, go straight. From the light, drive 0.1 miles (0.1 km) and go straight through a traffic circle with a statue, and in 0.4 miles (0.6 km) straight through the next circle. In 0.1 miles (0.1 km) there is a traffic "oval", take the 11:00 exit (not the 1:00 exit). Travel two miles (three km) to come to the end of the road. Turn left and then right at the stop sign at the next street. Stay on this main road, and in about 3.8 miles (six km) you will reach the park entrance. There will be a dirt parking area to your left.

Confused? No kidding. Almost none of the streets have signs, so street names are of little help. If you accidentally end up anywhere near the bullring, you should see signs pointing to the Natural Park. Good luck.

Doñana Natural Park Travel Notes:

El Bosque to Benamahoma:
Sierra de Grazalema Hike

In Sierra de Grazalema Natural Park there are quite a number of hiking trails to explore. Start your adventures on the closest one, walking the path leading from El Bosque to Benamahoma. This hike, the Sendero del Río Majaceite, follows the Majaceite River on a well-maintained, partly shaded trail. It starts out deceptively flat but becomes satisfyingly hilly. The trailhead map in El Bosque shows a distance of five kilometers to Benamahoma with a medium difficulty rating.

Travel time: About one hour 15 minutes to the trailhead.

Things to do in a day:

- ❑ Visit the Sierra de Grazalema Visitor's Center to get a map and see displays of the park. Open on Monday–Friday from 10:00–14:00, and weekends and holidays from 9:00–14:00. Also open Friday and Saturday afternoons from 16:00–18:00 in the winter and 18:00–20:00 in the summer. Phone: 956-72-7029. Public restrooms are located here.

- ❑ Hike five kilometers to Benamahoma. (Allow 1.5–2.0 hours)

- ❑ Relax with a cold drink on the shaded patio of Venta El Bujio in Benamahoma.

- ❑ Hike five kilometers back to El Bosque. (Allow 1.5–2.0 hours)

Food tips: If you need a meal before you hike, try Hostel Enrique Calvillo. It's located just down the street from the Visitor's Center, across the narrow bridge, and on the left. It's not inexpensive, but has good gazpacho and homemade bread. On the weekends the restaurant seems popular with hikers and locals alike. We found the fastest way to get service was to order at the bar. The *revueltos pata-*

tas con chorizo is like garlic fries, scrambled eggs, and chorizo sausage mixed together. Not quite carbo-loading, but filling.

In Benamahoma, the trail conveniently ends at the shaded patio of Venta El Bujio, a nice setting to enjoy your choice of a cold drink, a *tapa*, a full meal, or an ice cream.

Highlight: A hike with a cool mountain stream in the midst of flowering olean-der, fig trees, wildflowers, wild berries, butterflies, birds, trout, skinny brown liz-ards with long green tails, and the occasional rushing waterfall.

Lowlight: Drawing blood on one of the many thorny vines hanging overhead.

Sidelight: About 1.5 miles (2.4 km) from the trailhead, or two miles (3.2 km) from the main road, is a botanical garden, El Castillejo. If you're not too tired from your hike, stop by and visit. The garden is very enjoyable, with cobblestone trails, bubbling brooks, and colorful flowers. It's easy to spend half an hour or more walking the trail and enjoying the countryside. To get there, take the cob-blestone road up past the trailhead and follow signs to the botanical garden. Park 50 meters beyond the entrance in a dirt lot on the left, and walk back to the entrance gate. The gate may be shut, but not locked. Open it then shut it behind you. Open daily from 10:00–14:00 and 17:00–20:00. Free.

Hint: We saw some people in bathing suits in the Majaceite River, but I wouldn't recommend swimming there…it was downstream from the local family pig farm.

Directions: From Rota, drive towards Jerez on the A-491. At the casino/water park traffic circle take the 2:00 exit towards El Portal (CA-201). In six miles (10 km), when the road comes to a 'T' at a traffic circle, turn right onto the A-381. In one mile (1.6 km), take the A-4 north towards Sevilla. In three miles (five km) take the A-382 exit. Turn right towards Arcos de la Frontera. After driving about 15 miles (24 km), go straight through a number of stoplights. Central Arcos will be on your right. Just past Arcos, turn right onto the A-372. Signs point to Ubrique and El Bosque. Follow the A-372 approximately 18 miles (29 km) to El Bosque.

To get to the Visitor's Center, enter El Bosque. Go straight through the traffic circle, and in 0.1 miles (0.1 km) turn right at a small sign that reads "Punto de Información". Park just beyond the turnoff at the small traffic circle with the water wheel. Just down Avenida de la Disputación on the right is the Natural Park Information Center. Go through the doorway, straight back, and up the stairs to reach it.

To reach the trailhead, get back into your car. Backtrack from the water wheel, cross the A-372 intersection and follow signs to "Jardin Botanical". You will drive on a cobblestone road about 0.4 miles (0.6 km). The trailhead will be on your left marked by a sign that reads "Sendero Río Majaceite". Street parking can be found across the bridge just past the trailhead.

El Bosque Travel Notes:

El Portal—Kariba

Think you've seen everything within a 20-mile radius of Rota? Think again! Would you believe that located just outside El Portal is Kariba, a crocodile farm housing over 1000 crocodiles? Admittedly, it's a little pricey (2003 prices: 6 euros/adults, 4 euros/children), but quite fascinating with a fairly high creepy quotient. The farm is open July 1–September 30 from 17:00–21:00 every day. Not so much a day trip, but rather a summer evening adventure. So if you've got some time in Rota, go check it out! Where else would you get the chance to see so many crocodiles so close to home?

Travel time: About 30 minutes if you have to wait at the tracks in El Portal for a train to pass.

Things to do in a day:

- ❏ See tiny baby crocodiles crawling all over each other.

- ❏ See bigger baby crocodiles resting with their jaws wide open.

- ❏ See young juvenile crocodiles hissing in their pen.

- ❏ See huge adult crocodiles lazing by the water.

- ❏ Plan a little over an hour to see the crocodiles, walk a circular path around the natural setting of the adult pen, and see a feeding. If there are no crocodile eggs to view, you can ask to see an already hatched shell.

Food tip: The brochure lists a *merendero*, a picnic spot in the country. There are outdoor picnic tables and a soda machine, so bring some snacks.

Highlight: Definitely the crocodile feedings—especially the juveniles. The juvenile crocodiles appeared ravenous, snapping and hissing and crawling on top of each other to get their meal. Some performed the "death roll" with their chicken pieces, just to make sure those pieces were good and dead. You may never look at raw chicken the same way again.

Lowlight: Getting splashed with old, brackish crocodile water during the feeding frenzy.

Sidelight: Impress your kids with these crocodile facts:

1. Some members of the crocodile family can grow to be seven meters long and weigh 1000 kg.

2. The Nile crocodile lives in freshwater lakes, swamps, rivers, and coastal estuaries.

3. The crocodile is cold-blooded with a four-chamber heart.

4. The crocodile's jaws are strong enough to crush the bones of small animals.

5. In the wild, young crocodiles feed on insects on the land. As a sub-adult, they move to the water to eat fish, frogs, and small mammals. As an adult, they generally eat large fish but can ambush large game (zebras, antelope, and buffalo) at the water's edge.

6. The crocodile has 30 to 40 teeth in each jaw. The fourth tooth on each side of the lower jaw is exposed when the crocodile has its mouth shut; not so on an alligator.

7. The crocodile female lays her eggs (numbering 16 to 90, 40 average) buried in the sand, mud, or plant debris.

8. The crocodile spends much of its time in the water, using its tail to swim, but is a fast runner on land.

Hint: Small feedings occur every day, but Wednesdays are the largest feeding day of the week, with the main feeding occurring around 19:30–20:00. Since feeding time is definitely the highlight, you may want to call to verify the schedule (phone: 956-23-7468). Kariba's website (only in Spanish) is www. cocodrilosjerez.com and their e-mail address is info@cocodrilosjerez.com.

Directions: From Rota, drive towards Jerez on the A-491. At the casino/water park traffic circle take the 2:00 exit towards El Portal (CA-201). In 2.6 miles (4.2 km) on the El Portal road there will be a right hand turn, just before a stoplight.

Turn right, look both ways, and cross the railroad tracks. In 1.3 miles (2.1 km) there should be a hand-painted sign reading "Cocodrilos" pointing to the right. Turn right at this intersection, and in 4.1 miles (6.6 km) Kariba will be on your left. Take the unpaved road (that at times looks more like a dry riverbed) for 0.3 miles (0.5 km) to reach the farm.

El Portal Travel Notes:

El Portal—Yeguada de la Cartuja

El Portal is full of surprises. Located in the pastures on the outskirts of town is a horse breeding ranch, Yeguada de la Cartuja—Hierro del Bocado. This working ranch offers tours Saturday at 11:00 featuring the lovely Cartujano horse. A visit entails touring the grounds, visiting with the horses, and watching a performance in a modern indoor arena. All in all, a great day trip for horse lovers, kids, and guests.

Travel time: About 25 minutes.

Things to do in a day:

- ❏ Visit the grounds and see the stallions, one-year olds, two-year olds, the under one-year olds, the hospital, and the carriage house. (45-minute tours in English, Spanish, and German)

- ❏ Watch the show featuring free running horses, dressage, and carriage events. (One hour)

- ❏ Sip complimentary sherry and shop for gifts. (Allow 15 minutes)

Food tip: Bring snacks for the kids since the tour and show will span the American lunch hour. Plan to be finished sometime after 13:00.

Highlight: Getting up close and personal with so many beautiful horses.

Lowlight: A nip from a curious colt gave my husband a bruise on his forearm. Did I mention we were up close and personal?

Sidelight: Historically, the Carthusian Monastery has bred the Cartujano horse since the 15th century. Today, Yeguada de la Cartuja stud farm is considered to have the most important stock of Cartujano horses. Balanced movement, precise reactions, durability, fluidity, and energy characterize this noble horse. Check out www.yeguadacartuja.com for an in-depth history of the Cartujano horse.

Hint: It's a good idea to call in advance to see if you need reservations (956-16-2809). Yeguada de la Cartuja is well known on the "horse tourist" circuit and large tour buses can show up for the event.

Directions: From Rota, drive towards Jerez on the A-491. At the casino/water park traffic circle take the 2:00 exit towards El Portal (CA-201). In 2.6 miles (4.2 km) on the El Portal road there will be a right hand turn, just before a stoplight. There is a sign for Yeguada de la Cartuja. Turn right, look both ways, and cross the railroad tracks. Travel on this road 4.0 miles (6.4 km), go under a bridge, and the gates for Yeguada de la Cartuja will be on your left. Go through the gates and drive 0.3 miles (0.5 km) to reach the parking lot on your left. Buy your tickets from the kiosk here. 2004 prices: €10.

El Portal Travel Notes:

El Puerto de Santa María

Spend a day as a tourist in one of Naval Base Rota's hometowns. Head to El Puerto de Santa María on a Saturday morning to discover the best the city has to offer. "Puerto" draws visitors for the sherry, but the city has much more: historical churches, a medieval castle, and a fountain that used to supply fresh water to ships departing for the New World. Open your eyes to the local attractions and enjoy yourself in Puerto.

Travel time: About 15 minutes.

Things to do on a Saturday:

❑ Walk the "red line" historical route through Puerto. On your walk see one of the largest bullrings in Spain, seating 15,000 people. (<2 hours to walk the route)

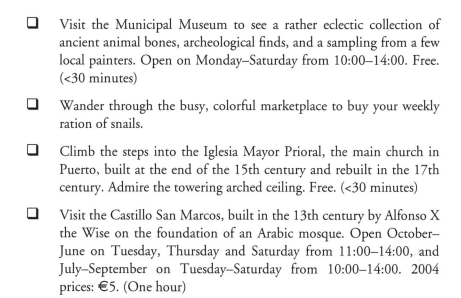

❑ Visit the Municipal Museum to see a rather eclectic collection of ancient animal bones, archeological finds, and a sampling from a few local painters. Open on Monday–Saturday from 10:00–14:00. Free. (<30 minutes)

❑ Wander through the busy, colorful marketplace to buy your weekly ration of snails.

❑ Climb the steps into the Iglesia Mayor Prioral, the main church in Puerto, built at the end of the 15th century and rebuilt in the 17th century. Admire the towering arched ceiling. Free. (<30 minutes)

❑ Visit the Castillo San Marcos, built in the 13th century by Alfonso X the Wise on the foundation of an Arabic mosque. Open October–June on Tuesday, Thursday and Saturday from 11:00–14:00, and July–September on Tuesday–Saturday from 10:00–14:00. 2004 prices: €5. (One hour)

Food tip: There are many restaurants in downtown Puerto to try. If you can ignore the street traffic, the restaurants running along the street next to the Guadalete River are popular and tasty. To dine like the locals, try Romerijo's and order your seafood at the counter and take it to the outdoor tables to enjoy with a drink. For a taste of the Middle East, go next door to Tele Showarma. A flatbread and hummus appetizer and showarma sandwich make a fine meal. If you prefer the Far East, try Restaurante Chino Hong Kong, down the street near the entrance to the parking lot. And for drinks or *tapas* on the sidewalk promenade, try Bar Santa María, located on the other side of the road near the amusement park rides.

Highlight: Being in the Iglesia Mayor Prioral the Saturday before Holy Week (Semana Santa). There was a palatable excitement in the air as people were streaming into the church to see how each Brotherhood's floats were being prepared for the procession the following week.

Lowlight: The streets are pretty busy in Puerto. There are usually quite a few cars out on a Saturday morning, and the noise from the racing mopeds rarely abates.

Sidelight: The true charm of El Puerto de Santa María lies in its local festivals and celebrations. Here is a sampling of some events that capture the heart of Puerto.

Carnavál: Carnavál is Spain's Mardi Gras celebration occurring just before the start of Lent in February. While Mardi Gras festivities typically last one day in the U.S., in Spain the carnavál celebrations have a habit of lasting for days or weeks.

The city of Cádiz is renown for its loud and raucous festival. They celebrated even during the time of Franco's suppression. Comparatively, Puerto's celebration is more like a hometown affair. Head here for a taste of the local.

The parade route generally starts at the bullring. Floats and bands all line up around the bullring waiting for the official start. When the parade starts, participants slowly proceed down Avenida del Ejercito to the delight of a rather unmanageable crowd. Just because the spectators start by lining up on the sidewalk, don't expect them to remain there. People will often (always) pool onto the street nullifying your front row spot. Just accept it, you can't change it.

There's definitely a party atmosphere as floats pass by with people dressed in costumes, children throwing streamers and candy, and drummers who make the air vibrate with the rat-a-tat-tat and booming drums.

Go early to find street parking.

Semana Santa: The processions during *Semana Santa* (Holy Week) are truly a "must-see" in Puerto. These events are incredible religious parades taking place daily between Palm Sunday and Easter Sunday. Individual *Hermanodads* (Brotherhoods) participate each day of the week, hand-carrying their own set of floats through the streets of town.

During the procession you will first see hooded penitents carrying tall candles. Children watching on the parade route will approach the penitents to ask for wax drippings for their growing ball of lucky candle wax. The younger penitents are generally very accommodating, the adults, not so accommodating.

A large float of Jesus depicts a scene from the time between Palm Sunday and Easter Sunday and is accompanied by music. Strong men hidden underneath carry these floats, shuffling through the cobblestone streets with only their feet visible. On Good Friday, women representing the mourners follow, dressed all in black and wearing *mantillas*, an ornate comb draped with lace in their hair.

The procession culminates with a float carrying a statue of the Virgin Mary. She wears a long flowing cloak and is lit up by dozens of tall white candles. The float, laden with silver, appears immensely heavy. The smell of incense mingles with music from the following marching band, lingering in the air as the procession moves past.

As with many religious festivals in Spain, there is a carnival-type atmosphere on the streets. Candy stands are open on street corners, vendors hawk bags of nuts through the crowd, and the carnival rides next to the river are open. Make sure you try the salty *patatas fritas* (potato chips), cut up and fried crisp right in front of you.

What is the best way to see this incredible procession? Start with a little planning. Visit the Tourist Information Office during the weeks preceding Semana Santa. They can provide a map and a timetable of when the Brotherhoods depart the first church and where the route takes them. Plan to go early in the evening. We had no trouble finding a front row spot on the route during the early part of the procession, and parking was easier. Maundy Thursday, Good Friday, and Easter Sunday are considered to be the week's highlights.

Feria: Puerto's feria is the annual spring fair traditionally held one week in May each year. It is a colorful and busy display of horses, amusement park rides, and games, as well as a place for women to showcase their elaborate feria dresses. The dresses you will see can be quite varied. Polka dots seem to be the main choice of pattern, but you can also see striped or floral dresses or a combination of the above. Above all, there will be ruffles. And when the women gather in large circles to sing and dance, have your camera ready for this swirling riot of colors.

The dancing, Sevillana style, often breaks out spontaneously on the street, or in the *casetas*, temporary stalls set up for enjoying food and drink. Sevillana dancing is most recognized by the graceful movement of the arms and hands, moving in rhythm to singing, clapping, and guitar. Enjoy a traditional sherry while you watch this joyful dancing.

During the feria season, even the horses dress for the celebrations. In Puerto, you will see horses with colorful pom-pom ball decorations about their faces and manes, adorned with jingling bells and pulling shiny carriages.

When you are ready for a little excitement, try your hand at the carnival games or ride the amusement park rides. If you see a mini-roller coaster, water ride, or bumper car ride you'd like to try, buy individual tickets from the ticket booth associated with that ride. When you've had enough sun, ice cream, and rides, call it a day and head back to your car.

The feria grounds are located just off the A-491. From Rota, drive in the direction of Jerez on the A-491. Take the CA-602 El Puerto-Sanlúcar exit and turn left. The feria grounds will immediately be on your right. There is a huge, pay, dirt parking lot on your left. Enjoy!

Bullfighting: It is said if you haven't see the bulls in El Puerto de Santa María, you don't know bullfighting. The bullfight is an elaborate and deadly encounter between man and beast, but it may not be to everyone's liking. It's helpful to watch a bullfight on Spanish television before attending an event. You will become more familiar with the event, and slightly desensitized to the inevitable appearance of blood.

The bullfighting season officially opens after April Feria, and ends early September. Fights are typically held on Sunday evenings starting at 19:00 and are also occasionally held Friday nights in the summer. You will see posters go up all around town advertising the details. The event generally takes under three hours.

A bullfight is full of tradition and pageantry. Here's an idea of what you might expect at a classic bullfight. Three matadors will face six bulls. From birth these bulls have been raised for the fight and tested for their aggressiveness. At the start of each fight a man will enter the ring with a board displaying the name of the bull, the ranch where he was raised, and his massive weight.

The fight commences when the bull enters the ring. The matador and other brave men, called *capeadores*, attempt to initially tire the bull by making him charge their capes. As the bull passes dangerously close, prepare to shout, "Olé!" with the other spectators.

Trumpets will announce the first change. Men called *picadors*, riding blind-folded horses, come out and attempt to jab the bull on the back of his neck with long lances. The bull often tries to gore the horse during this procedure. Don't worry; even if the horse gets knocked down and lies motionless with his legs curled up in a "fetal" position, he should be fine. He has protective, thick padding all over his body. The worst damage we saw when a horse was knocked over was the *picador's* pants ripped down the backside.

Trumpets will again announce the next change of events. *Banderilleros*, men on foot carrying *banderillas* (spears with ribbons), face the bull. They attempt to jab six spears into the bull, two at a time. The *banderillas* that are properly placed will remain dangling from the bull's neck, and you'll probably start to notice the blood at this point in the fight.

The trumpets sound again to announce the highlight of the fight, when the matador goes solo into the ring. The matador, wearing traditional pink socks with his sequined outfit, enters the ring with a sword and cape. While the bull charges after the cape, the matador postures, struts, and curls his lip. He wipes his sword on the bulls flank and has the affront to turn his back on the dangerous beast and saunter away. It's a carefully orchestrated display designed to showcase the matador's attitude and bravery. (I can only imagine the aspiring young matador practicing his lip curl in front of the mirror at home.)

After the bull tires and has shown his valor, the matador exchanges his sword and the crowd quiets. The matador stares the bull down and attempts to bury the sword to the hilt into the top of the bull's neck. If it doesn't go in the first time, he tries again. Once the sword is in, the bull is made to run until he drops, at which point a small dagger is jabbed into his head. If the bull continues to run despite efforts to make him drop, the matador will use a special sword instead of the dagger to finish the bull off.

A horse arrives to drag the bull out of the ring. The crowd will clap if the bull has shown his valor, and whistle if the bull didn't perform up to the traditional standards of fearless Andalucían bulls.

If the crowd liked the matador, they will wave white handkerchiefs and the president will award the matador with the bull's ear. He will award a second ear, or possibly the tail, if both the matador and bull showed remarkable courage. Yes, historically there have been bulls spared from death because of their incredible valor, but if you talk to a Spaniard, they'll be pressed to come up with the time that last happened. The matador may do a "lap of glory" around the ring after the fight, and spectators will throw their hat or fan for him to touch and throw back. Watch out, he may also throw the ear he just earned into the crowd!

Here are some hints on seeing a bullfight in Puerto. Go early in the week to buy your tickets. The ticket booth located in the bullring is open during the week prior to the fight. The *sombra* (shade) seats are more expensive than the *sol* (sun) seats, and the summer sun doesn't drop below the stadium until after 20:30. The seats are stadium benches, with no backrests. Parking is easy if you park in one of the dirt parking lots next to the river and walk the short distance back to the bullring. If you want to park at the bullring, go early. Make sure you get to the bullfight on time, and don't get up from your seat during the fight. You can bring in food, and there's beer and water for sale in the stadium. Live music punctuates the evening. Essentially, you'll do fine if you remember just one rule…don't root for the bull.

August Book Fair: If you love books or you're studying Spanish and need some extra materials, make a point to see the book fair in August. Temporary bookstalls open up late evening, around 20:00, along the walkway next to the river. These stands sell an eclectic mix including children's books, cookbooks, and picture books. There are carnival rides and food stands open to complete the lively atmosphere. Shop and browse during a pleasant summer's evening stroll.

Hints:

1. At the marketplace, buy *margarita* (daisy) flowers for blooms that stay fresh for weeks.

2. Go by the castle before starting your walk to check on the time for the English tour, and then show up early. We were originally told our tour was at 13:00, but the time moved to 12:30 while we were on our walk.

3. If possible, plan to do the castle tour after walking the "red line" route since the tour included a surprise sherry and brandy tasting at the end. After tasting on an empty stomach, you might not be as motivated to hike through the rest of the city.

Directions: Leaving Naval Base Rota base by the Puerto gate, turn left on the CA-603 to head to El Puerto de Santa María. You will go through a number of traffic circles. At the traffic circle in about 5.0 miles (eight km) take the 11:00 exit following signs to "centro ciudad". Get in the right lane and bear right in 0.2 miles (0.3 km). In 0.1 miles (0.1 km) take the 1:00 exit at the traffic circle. Drive about 0.7 miles (1.1 km) passing the bullring and *bodega* (winery) warehouses. At the 'T' intersection turn left and drive parallel to the river for about 0.4 miles (0.6 km). There is a cobblestone pay parking lot at the bend in the road to the right.

After you park, walk up Calle Luna, perpendicular to the river. The Tourist Information Office is located up a block and a half on the right. Pick up a map and other information about current festivals and exhibits here.

El Puerto de Santa María Travel Notes:

Gibraltar

Grab your passport and take a trip to a corner of the Great British Empire. Britain still claims ownership of this small peninsula, but Spain would love to have it back. It's a strategic area that has been fought over for centuries, but for the traveler, it makes for a great day trip. Depart Spain and cross the border to Gibraltar to get a taste of England—only much sunnier. Cheerio!

Travel time: About one hour 40 minutes.

Things to do in a day:

❏ Hop on the cable car and ride to the top of The Rock. The cable car is open daily from 9:30–17:15; the last car down is at 17:45. Make sure your ticket includes Saint Michael's Cave, which is open until 18:30. 2004 prices: £29 for two people (roughly 26 dollars per person) for roundtrip tickets on the cable car that also includes a visit to the cave. A one-way trip on the cable car without the cave ran €10 and a roundtrip ride without the cave was €12.50. Credit cards, euros, and pounds accepted.

   • Once on top of The Rock, make sure you take in the views from the summit at the cable car stop. There are great views of the Mediterranean, Atlantic, and Morocco. (Allow 10–20 minutes)

   • Hike over to Saint Michael's Cave to see massive stalactites, stalagmites, and displays about the history of the cave. (Allow 30–45 minutes, more if you are enjoying the cool air on a hot day)

   • The Barbary ape makes its home on The Rock. You'll no doubt see plenty of apes on your walk to the cave. Watch out, they like to steal things. (Allow 10–20 minutes to see the apes and get some photos)

- From the cave, hike midway down to the Ape's Den and catch the cable car down from here. (10–15 minutes)

- If you have time and like to hike, then other items that may interest you include the Great Siege Tunnels and the Moorish castle, although it makes for quite a long walk to see everything and then hike down in the summer heat, trust me.

- Another way to see The Rock is by taxi or minibus. The drivers assured us the prices were the same as the cable car ride, and that you'd actually see more since you wouldn't have to walk all of it. Friends of ours have enjoyed that route, but we preferred to set our own pace and get some exercise.

❑ Wander through the Gibraltar Botanic Gardens, located right next to the cable car station at the base. The gardens were opened in 1816. Take a stroll down meandering trails past exotic plants, flowers, and waterscapes. Free. (Allow 30 minutes)

❑ Take a stroll, heading back towards the border. Detour into Trafalgar Cemetery, then walk to Main Street to reach the pedestrian shopping zone. You'll find all things British, including a Marks & Spencer department store. Most shops close at 19:00 on weekdays, 17:00 on Saturdays, and 14:00 on Sundays. Keep walking to the end of Main Street to reach Casemates Square, a historic cobblestone square. (Allow 30 minutes to make the walk to the end and window shop)

Food tip: There are some food options on Main Street, but Casemates Square is a good bet. You can find Burger King and Pizza Hut if you must, but there are some great little pubs serving tasty Indian food and the British staple, fish and chips. Find what suits your tastes and enjoy your meal seated under umbrellas in the square.

Highlight: Everything about The Rock: the views, the apes, and the cave.

Lowlight: Forgetting to save a Gibraltar pound. An authentic Gibraltar pound would have made a nice addition to my small coin collection.

Sidelight: Philatelists, you're in luck. Gibraltar is a hotbed of stamp collecting. Every little shop seems to have an assortment of stamps to peruse through. We don't even collect stamps and we ended up walking away with some as a rather expensive memento. You can visit www.gibraltar-stamps.com to see what they have to offer.

Hints:

1. Don't forget your passport; you're entering a different country.

2. There are very few signs indicating you're approaching the Gibraltar exit on the A-7/E-15 until just before your turnoff. It's probably resulting from remnant animosity stemming from the time the British were ceded Gibraltar by the Treaty of Utrecht in 1713.

3. We found we didn't need to exchange euros for pounds as most shops and restaurants took both.

4. You should be able to pick up a free map at an Information Desk as you cross the border into Gibraltar.

Directions: Take the inland route to save time. From Rota, drive towards Jerez on the A-491, and at the casino/water park traffic circle take the 2:00 exit towards El Portal (CA-201). In six miles (10 km), when the road comes to a 'T' at a traffic circle, turn right onto the A-381. Travel on this road for about 54 miles (87 km), passing Los Barrios, until the road intersects with the A-7/E-15. Turn east towards Gibraltar, Malaga, and San Roque. Travel on the A-7/E-15 for about 4.5 miles (7.3 km) to get to the Gibraltar exit. Follow this road straight about 4.5 miles (7.3 km). Stay in the left lane to stay in Spain, the right lane will enter Gibraltar. To park on the Spanish side, one option is to pass the Gibraltar border on your right, and take a left hand turn 0.1 miles (0.1 km) further on. There will be a McDonalds on your left. There is pay parking all along this street. Locate the meter to buy a parking ticket, put in your euro coins and take out your ticket (2004 prices: €4 for 5 hours of parking). Put your ticket in your car, visible on your dashboard.

Walk back to the Gibraltar border, cross the border showing your passport, and wait at the bus stop for bus #3 to take you into town. The buses run about every 15–20 minutes and take euros so you don't have to worry about carrying pounds. (2004 prices: €1.50 for a round trip, unlimited day use €2.50.) Bus #3 will take you all the way to The Rock's cable car.

You can also drive across the border and find parking at the cable car parking lot, but if you didn't get stuck in border traffic coming over, you may get stuck in border traffic going back. Don't count on off-season travel to make border crossings easier. Unless you're staying overnight in a hotel, park on the Spanish side.

Gibraltar Travel Notes:

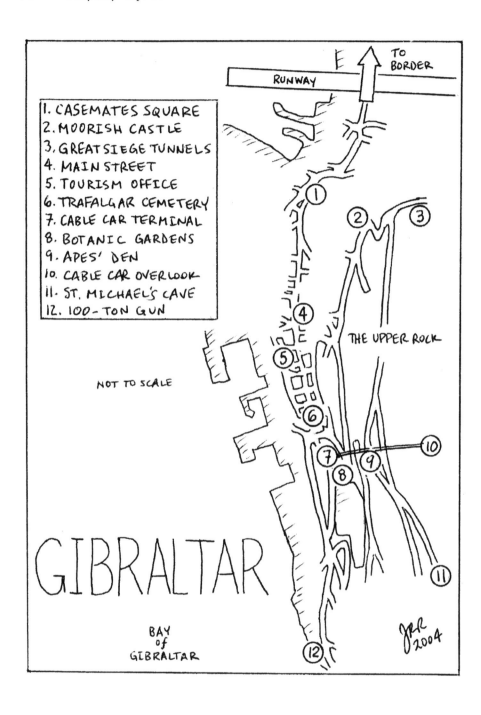

1. CASEMATES SQUARE
2. MOORISH CASTLE
3. GREAT SIEGE TUNNELS
4. MAIN STREET
5. TOURISM OFFICE
6. TRAFALGAR CEMETERY
7. CABLE CAR TERMINAL
8. BOTANIC GARDENS
9. APES' DEN
10. CABLE CAR OVERLOOK
11. ST. MICHAEL'S CAVE
12. 100-TON GUN

RUNWAY

TO BORDER

THE UPPER ROCK

NOT TO SCALE

GIBRALTAR

BAY of GIBRALTAR

2004

Granada

Granada is an old, beautiful city featuring the Alhambra, an extensive Moorish fortress and palace. La Alhambra perches on a hilltop and offers views of the city below and the mountains above. The city also offers a noteworthy Cathedral and Royal Chapel. Granada is included in this book in case some of you are actually tempted to visit the city as a day trip. Realistically, this city needs an overnight stay simply because it takes about four hours to get to Granada from Rota. If you do it in a day, you'll have time to visit La Alhambra and not much else. If you stay overnight, a few other sites worth visiting are mentioned.

Travel time: About four hours if you make two quick stops, detour to avoid an accident scene, miss an exit, and don't hit rush-hour traffic…but give yourself some extra time.

Things to do in a day:

❑   Explore La Alhambra. Open March–October from 8:30–20:00, and November–February from 8:30–18:00. 2004 prices: €10 for adults, children under 8 are free. It will take about five hours to do it justice.

  •   Palacios Nazaries. Your ticket to La Alhambra will have an entry time for the palace and you will have a half hour window to enter the Palace. The Palace is the highlight, so do *not* miss your entry time! (Allow one hour)

  •   Alcazaba, the old fortress. Climb all the stairs, admire the views, and look for some good photo ops. (Allow one hour)

  •   Charles V palace. Wander through the columns, enjoy the view from the second level, and check out the free museum on the ground level. (Allow one hour)

  •   Generalife Gardens. Admire the fountains and gardens, beautiful year round. (Allow one hour)

Things to do the next day:

❑   Visit the Royal Chapel (connected to the cathedral) that contains King Ferdinand and Queen Isabel's tombs and the royal treasury. Open October–March on Monday–Saturday from 10:30–13:00 and 15:30–18:30, closed Sunday. Open April–September on Monday–Saturday from 10:30–13:00 and 16:00–19:00, and Sunday from 11:00–13:00 and 16:00–19:00. 2003 prices: €2.50. (Allow one hour)

❑   Wander through Granada's Cathedral. Pick your favorite description: impressive, grandiose, beautiful, light, or airy. Open October–March on Monday–Saturday from 10:30–13:00, closed Sunday. Open April–September on Monday–Saturday from 10:30–13:00 and 16:00–19:00, and Sunday from 16:00–19:00. 2003 prices: €2.50. (Allow one hour)

❑   Enjoy the vistas from the overlook at the San Nicolas Mirador. Share sensational views of the Alhambra and the mountain backdrop with half the dreadlock population of Granada, then turn around and wander through the narrow streets of the old Moorish Quarter. (One hour to admire and wander)

Food tips: It's advisable to bring food into the Alhambra since your selection once inside is limited. The Parador (state-run hotel) within the old walls has an expensive restaurant open during typical Spanish hours. There are vending machines with packaged food near the restrooms and a little kiosk selling drinks in the patio near the Alcazaba entrance. That's it for food selection within the walls.

If you want to treat yourself to a nice dinner, try Hotel Guadelupe 50 meters from the entrance of La Alhambra (Paseo de la Sabica, s/n Alhambra, www. hotelguadelupe.es). We splurged on Thanksgiving dinner in the hotel's restaurant and highly recommend the smoked salmon with capers and shavings of Parmesan, roasted duck with raspberry sauce, grilled pork tenderloin with vegetables, and tiramisu. I couldn't tell you about the German chocolate cake since my husband didn't offer me a taste. A little pricey with the tip and a bottle of wine, but well worth it!

Highlight: The Patio de Los Leones in La Alhambra's Palacios Nazarines—jammed with tourists but gorgeous. Buy a few postcards so you have pictures without all the tour groups mucking up your photos.

Lowlight: Spending over 30 minutes looking for the "comfort blanket" dropped by our toddler in the gardens of La Alhambra's Generalife. Luckily, we found it only to nearly lose it again the next day at a city bus stop. Imagine trying to ask the Spanish bus driver to "please stop the bus because our baby's Very Important Blanket was lying on the sidewalk back at the bus stop." He must have understood our cries because he stopped in the middle of traffic and opened the back door, enabling me to leap across three lanes to rescue it.

Sidelights: Granada is the launching point for skiing in the Spanish Sierra Nevadas. It takes about one hour to drive from the city to the ski area on winding, mountain roads. While there are no great ski lodge hangout areas for non-smoking non-skiers at the ski area, on a clear day you are supposed to be able to see Morocco from the summit, and that's pretty cool.

Washington Irving's book, *Tales of the Alhambra*, was written while he was staying within the old walls of the Moorish fortress. Pick up a copy before your trip to travel back in time.

Hints:

1. No doubt you've heard it before, but it can't be stressed enough…make advance reservations for the Alhambra visit. Call BBVA at 902-22-4460, English spoken, or try the website www.Alhambratickets.com, also in English. A small booking fee is charged and well worth it (2004 fee: €0.88 per ticket). Make sure each person is ticketed, including the children. In November we were able to make reservations the same week we visited, but the word is in the summer it's a different story.

2. Rent an audio-guide at the entrance to La Alhambra (2003 prices: about €3 each and you need one for each person). The audio-guide provides history as well as a little gossip on romantic liaisons, murders, and famous authors and is recommended to get the most out of your tour.

3. Avoid having to sprint through La Alhambra's grounds to make your palace entry time. Arrive at least an hour in advance before your entry time to account for ticket lines, audio-guide lines, and a ten-minute walk to the Palaces. No doubt you will see people racing through the crowds trying to make their entrance times!

Directions: From Rota, drive towards Jerez on the A-491. At the casino/water park traffic circle take the 2:00 exit towards El Portal (CA-201). In six miles (10 km), when the road comes to a 'T' at a traffic circle, turn right onto the A-381. In one mile (1.6 km), take the A-4 north to Sevilla. In three miles (five km), take the A-382 exit. Turn right towards Arcos de la Frontera. Follow the A-382 for about 98 miles (158 km). Take the A-92 towards Granada. Follow signs towards Granada and in about one hour take the marked exit to Granada. From there, get on the Circunvalación road, N-323, towards Granada's city center.

To reach La Alhambra, take the marked exit off the Circunvalación road and follow the numerous signs to the Alhambra's pay parking lots.

To reach the city center and the cathedral, follow the Circunvalación road back towards the A-92 and take exit Centro Recogidas, towards the city center. Then it's nearly two miles (3.2 km) to the city center. As soon as you see a sign for a parking garage, *any* parking garage, take it and then ask someone for directions to the cathedral. We wound around and parked at the Puerto Real Parking Garage and enjoyed a brisk walk past the shops to the cathedral. The downtown area is full of one-way streets and tall buildings so detailed directions to get to parking are near impossible! If you are staying overnight in the city, consider a taxi to avoid the headache of city driving.

To reach the San Nicolas Mirador, exit the cathedral and turn to the right. A few yards down the street you will see a bus stop. Take bus #31 that may or may not wind through the Sacremonte part of town before proceeding to San Nicolas. To return, catch the same bus to loop back to the cathedral. 2003 bus prices: €0.85.

Returning to Rota on the A-92, the exit for the A-382 was not marked. Exit #146 to Antequera is also the A-382 to Arcos.

Granada Travel Notes:

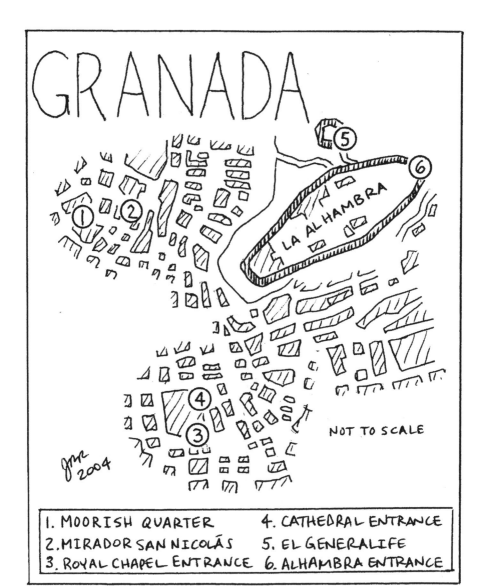

1. MOORISH QUARTER   4. CATHEDRAL ENTRANCE
2. MIRADOR SAN NICOLÁS   5. EL GENERALIFE
3. ROYAL CHAPEL ENTRANCE   6. ALHAMBRA ENTRANCE

Grazalema

Grazalema is a small, whitewashed village that clings to the hillside in the mountains of the Sierra de la Grazalema. The village has plenty of beautiful old churches and panoramic views to admire, and it offers a free-access hike through the Sierra de Grazalema Natural Park. Come for the hiking and stay for the charm of an alpine *pueblo blanco* (white village).

Travel time: About one hour 50 minutes.

Things to do in a day:

❑ Hike the Sendero Camino de los Charcones. The hike is listed at 1.8 km (one mile) and 30 minutes one way. The trail takes you along a small mountain stream up to the lookout, Puerto de El Boyar Mirador, you passed on your drive into town. The hike is listed as a low-level difficulty, but it was all uphill going out, and all downhill coming back. The trip up to the *mirador* took us longer than 30 minutes, and I would hesitate in calling the difficulty "low". (Allow 1.5 hours up and back, especially since your car will be parked further down the road)

❑ Hit the city for some sightseeing. Walk to the main plaza, explore the cobblestone streets, check out the town vistas, and peek over the shoulders of local artists sketching and painting the small, quaint plazas. (Allow 1–2 hours)

❑ Do a little shopping. Grazalema is known for its handmade woolen items. The wool is crafted with hand-worked looms in the traditional method, read: expensive. 2004 prices: large blankets ran €83, elegant shawls were €88, and long scarves were €45. If you are in the main square and the Tourist Information Office is open, go upstairs. They have a one-stop shopping experience. You can find Grazalema walking sticks, woolen items, purses, and local cheeses and wines. The

Tourist Information Office is open on Tuesday–Sunday from 10:00–14:00 and 17:00–19:00.

Food tip: El Tajo Restaurante Taberna is conveniently located across from the city parking lot and boasts gorgeous views. Of course, they were closed for vacation when we tried visiting in late May 2004. We made do with a picnic lunch en route, and drinks and *tapas* on the main square after our hike.

Highlight: A nice hike that gave a taste of the outdoors but was short enough to allow time to explore the village.

Lowlight: I guess we took those winding mountain roads a little too fast…our toddler got carsick in the backseat.

Sidelight: If you have friends who enjoy hiking, here's an idea that looks like fun, but we haven't tried it yet.

There's a free access walk that runs between the Puerto del Boyar Mirador outside of Grazalema to Benaocaz, a white village to the south. The route, Sendero del Salto Cabrero, is a little over seven kilometers with a medium difficulty rating when hiking from Grazalema. The *mirador* and trailhead have an elevation of about 1100 meters (3600 feet), and during the hike the trail drops to an elevation of 800 meters (2600 feet) before climbing back to 900 meters (2950 feet) at Benaocaz. The hike in this direction is listed as taking between three and four hours. If you hike from the other direction, starting in Benaocaz, the hike will be harder as there is more uphill travel.

If doing this hike as a separate day trip, we recommend you call your hiking friends and caravan to El Bosque. From there, send one car to the Benaocaz trailhead and one car to the trailhead at the *mirador* (or slightly further to the Camping Tajo Rodillo parking lot in Grazalema). Start the hike and hopefully meet your hiking companions somewhere on the trail to exchange car keys (or carry a second set). After reaching the end of the trail, locate your friend's car and drive back to El Bosque to rendezvous at a previously agreed upon location. Cold drinks and *tapas* should no doubt round out the day. Of course, carry plenty of water, snacks, an emergency space blanket, first aid items, and a mobile phone.

If this sounds like fun, do some planning, make sure you can find the Benaocaz trailhead, and call your friends for a day of mountain air, stunning views, and healthy exercise.

Hints:

1. While driving to Grazalema, watch out for bicyclists flying down the winding mountain roads between Grazalema and El Bosque.

2. Don't expect oncoming traffic to slow down or give an inch. Drive defensively on those narrow roads.

3. The Sendero de los Charcones trail has quite a bit of gravel. Hiking boots are a better choice than sport sandals.

4. We saw an older gentleman hiking with an umbrella. He looked more prepared than we were for an unexpected mountain shower.

5. Grazalema is in the mountains. It will probably be cooler and cloudier than on the coast. Bring layers and consider raingear.

Directions: From Rota, drive towards Jerez on the A-491. At the casino/water park traffic circle take the 2:00 exit towards El Portal (CA-201). In six miles (10 km), when the road comes to a 'T' at a traffic circle, turn right onto the A-381. In one mile (1.6 km), take the A-4 north towards Sevilla. In three miles (five km) take exit A-382. Turn right towards Arcos de la Frontera. After driving about 15 miles (24 km), go straight through a number of stoplights. Central Arcos will be on your right. Just past the city, turn right onto the A-372. Signs point to Ubrique and El Bosque. Follow the A-372 approximately 18 miles (29 km) to El Bosque. Drive through the village of El Bosque following signs to Grazalema. Just outside of El Bosque, look for the road to take a left. Continue following signs to Grazalema. The road between El Bosque and Grazalema is twisty, winding, and slow. About 10 miles (16 km) past El Bosque (30 minutes), turn right to Grazalema.

To reach the trailhead, after your right hand turn, in about 0.5 miles (0.8 km) there will be a parking lot for Camping Tajo Rodillo. Park here and hike back up the road 0.2 miles (0.3 km) to reach the trailhead on your left.

To reach the village, keep driving and you will pass the town on your left. About one mile (1.6 km) from the camping parking lot you will be on the far edge of the village. You will find an upper parking lot, and just past that, a lower parking lot, both on your left. Park here to explore the village. Walk down the street about five minutes to reach the main square and explore. The town is small enough you probably won't need a map.

Grazalema Travel Notes:

Italica

Italica, located just north of Sevilla, was an ancient Roman city founded in 206 B.C. While much of the area has yet to be excavated, Italica is a place where you can see the Roman footprint in Andalucía without Moorish and modern structures built over it. Most of the city has been raided for building materials, but you can still see the theater, the amphitheater, and intricate mosaics crafted on the foundations of the city.

Travel time: About one hour 30 minutes, but your travel time may be faster as we were stuck on a side road behind a slow-moving horse-drawn trailer for some time.

Things to do in a day:

- ❑ Admire the Roman theater from the *mirador* lookout in the town of Santiponce. (See hint and directions.)

- ❑ Stroll through the Roman Amphitheater inside Italica and let your imagination provide the dramatic sounds of gladiators and wild animals.

- ❑ Wander through the remains of the city for a look at wide Roman streets, mosaics, thermal baths, and a floor plan of the houses. Italica is open April–September on Tuesday–Saturday from 8:30–20:30, and October–March on Tuesday–Saturday from 9:00–17:30. Open Sunday and holidays from 10:00–16:00. Closed Monday. 2004 prices: €1.50 per person, free to EU citizens. (Allow 1.5–2 hours)

Food tip: There's no food available in Italica, but there are some nice looking *ventas* (small restaurants) located outside the gates on the other side of the street.

If you are driving up on a Saturday in January and see a McDonalds next to a Leroy Merlin, cinema, and El Corte Inglés in a commercial center outside of Sevilla, and you think your toddler may need a lunch break, for heaven's sake reconsider! During the January sale season, this may qualify as the most poorly designed parking area in all of Spain.

Highlight: Admiring 2000-year old mosaics in shorts-weather in January.

Lowlight: Not getting to enjoy the good-looking *ventas* outside Italica's entrance due to bad timing and a sleeping baby.

Sidelight: If you are interested in archeological treasures, visit the Museo Arqueológico in Sevilla where much of what has been uncovered in Italica is displayed. The museum is located at the far end of the Parque de María Luisa in a pavilion built for the 1929 Exposition. Open on Tuesday from 15:00–20:00; Wednesday–Saturday from 9:00–20:00; and Sunday from 9:00–14:00. Closed Monday. 2004 prices: €1.50.

Hint: If you reach the lookout for the Roman Theater and it's gated shut, you can still take a peek from a side street. Walking from the *mirador* parking area, go past the street Jose Romero Velazquez, and before you reach the sign reading "Siete Revueltas", turn right and follow the street to the end where you will find a side view of the Theater.

Directions: From Rota, drive towards Jerez on the A-491. At the casino/water park traffic circle take the 2:00 exit towards El Portal (CA-201). In six miles (10 km), when the road comes to a 'T' at a traffic circle, turn right onto the A-381. In one mile (1.6 km), take the A-4 north to Sevilla. As you approach Sevilla, follow the signs towards Mérida on the A-66/E-803. You will be traveling northwest of Sevilla's city center. Roughly 75 miles (121 km) from Rota you will turn off the A-66/E-803 to Santiponce, and there will be a sign for Italica. Turn left at the intersection, right at the first traffic circle and follow the signs to Italica and the Roman Theater. In 0.5 miles (0.8 km) from the traffic circle bear right towards the Theater, and in another 0.5 miles (0.8 km) you'll reach the *mirador* for the Roman Theater. Park in the *mirador* parking lot and walk up the hill to see the theater. Continue driving on the main road through Santiponce approximately 0.5 more miles (0.8 km) to reach Italica. Park on the street on your right, pay the attendant to watch your car, and Italica will be on your left.

Italica Travel Notes:

Jerez I

Looking for something to do on a Sunday? Try these two ideas in Jerez: the González Byass bodega (winery) and the Jerez Zoo. Close enough for a Sunday outing or two without having to commit to an all-day affair. There are many local bodega tours from which to choose, but González Byass is highlighted for ease of the weekend traveler. They offer tours on Sundays, have established times for English tours, and don't require reservations.

Travel Time: About 25 minutes.

Things to do in a day:

- ❑ Visit the González Byass bodega to see how world-famous sherry is made. Tours in English are conducted Monday–Saturday at 11:30, 12:30, 13:30, 14:00, 15:30 16:30 and 17:30. (In summers the 15:30 tour is replaced by an 18:30 tour.) Sunday tours are scheduled at 11:30, 12:30, and 13:30. Call 956-35-7016 to verify the schedule. 2004 prices: €7. (Tours last about 1–1.5 hours depending on your sherry tasting and shopping habits)

- ❑ Drink sherry.

- ❑ Watch mice drink sherry.

- ❑ Watch strangers drink sherry.

- ❑ Visit the Jerez Zoo. Lions, tigers, and bats, oh my! Open in the winter from 10:00–18:00, and in the summer from 10:00–20:00. Closed Monday. 2004 prices: €4 for adults, €2.60 for children aged 3–13, free for children 2 and under. (Stroll through the wide variety of exhibits in a leisurely 1.5–2 hours)

Food Tip: Craving American food? There's a Pizza Hut located in Jerez. You can wind your way through town or follow the directions below.

Highlight: Discovering the zoo is actually much nicer than most guidebooks would have you believe.

Lowlight: Well, let's face it; the Jerez Zoo is not the World Famous San Diego Zoo.

Sidelights: Exit the González Byass bodega tour and straight ahead is the pretty church, Iglesia Catedral. Doors should be open on a Sunday to visit.

If you show up early for your bodega tour, you may be interested in touring the Jerez Alcázar while you wait. You can see the mosque, an oil mill, gardens, Arab baths, and the defensive gates. This fortress palace is located next to both the bodega and cathedral. Open daily in the summer from 10:00–20:00, and in the winter from 10:00–18:00. A small fee is charged.

Hint: The excellent González Byass 30-year old sherry is sold only at the bodega and at select wine shops in Spain. It's not exported, so enjoy it now. Ask for the very old (*muy viejo*) sherry, currently available in black cylindrical containers.

Directions: To González Byass, take the A-491 from Rota to the N-IV to Jerez. Take the first "centro ciudad" exit into Jerez (a large Carrefour will be on your right). The exit feeds you into a traffic circle; take the 12:00 exit towards the city center. Follow the road straight through another traffic circle and a traffic light. You will see the González Byass bodega on your left at Calle Manuel María González 12. Just past the bodega on the left is an underground parking garage, 0.5 miles (0.8 km) from the N-IV exit.

To get to the zoo, continue north on the N-IV past the González Byass exit. In 1.5 miles (2.4 km) there will be a hospital on your left. Take the road to the right across from the hospital. Signs point to "hospital", "Trebujena", and "centro ciudad". At the next intersection, turn right. Avenida de Trebujena becomes Avenida de la Serrana. Follow the road 0.2 miles (0.3 km). Turn right at Avenida San Juan Bosco. Follow Avenida San Juan Bosco 0.3 miles (0.5 km) until the road ends at the entrance to the zoo on Calle Taxdirt. Take a left and look for a dirt parking lot on your right. There may be a parking attendant to pay depending on the season.

To reach the Pizza Hut in town, get back on the N-IV traveling north and take the next traffic circle after the zoo exit, about 0.3 miles (0.5 km) further with a Bodegas Garvey building on your left. Take the 12:00 exit on the traffic circle and follow Avenida José de Carranza one mile (1.6 km). Turn right at the traffic circle onto Avenida Alcalde Álvaro (the Jerez fairgrounds will be on your left). Follow this street about one mile (1.6 km) and it will become Calle Sevilla. Pizza Hut will be on your left, Calle Sevilla 42. Drive straight ahead and circle around the plaza with a fountain, large pool, and carriage statue to find an underground parking garage.

Jerez Travel Notes:

1. GONZÁLEZ BYASS BODEGA
2. ALCÁZAR Y MEZQUITA
3. CATHEDRAL
4. BULLRING
5. PIZZA HUT
6. BAR LOS CISNES
7. CARRIAGE MUSEUM
8. SÁNDEMAN BODEGA
9. REAL ESCUELA
10. FERIA GROUNDS

TO ZOO

JEREZ
DE LA FRONTERA   I, II

TO TRAIN STATION

TO ROTA

NOT TO SCALE

2004

Jerez II

If you have a weekday free, head up to Jerez to experience what Jerez is famous for—horses and sherry. In one stop you can get a taste of both. The Real Escuela Andaluza del Arte Ecuestre (Royal Andalucían School of Equestrian Art) has horses famous for their dancing skills, and just around the corner from the school you can visit the famous Sandeman Bodega. See beautiful horses, sip some sherry, have a nice lunch, and call it a day trip.

Travel time: About 25 minutes.

Things to do in a day:

- ❏ Watch the famous dancing horses of Andalucía at the Royal Andalucían School of Equestrian Art. Tour the stables and tack room. Enjoy a show on Thursday or a less expensive practice session on Monday, Tuesday (in winter), Wednesday, or Friday. Buy your ticket at the gate and head toward the indoor arena in the large building on your left. Practice sessions generally run from 11:00–13:00, and the Thursday show starts at 12:00. From March–October shows also run on Tuesday at 12:00. Call 956-31-9635 or 956-31-8008 for the current schedule, or visit www.realescuela.org. During the practice session, periodic guided tours in English take you from the arena to the stables. 2004 prices: practice sessions are €6 for adults and €3 for children under 12; the show prices range from €13–21 for adults and €6–7.80 for children under 12. (Allow 1–2 hours)

- ❏ Visit the Sandeman Bodega and take a detailed and informative tour of the sherry-making process—naturally, a tasting is included. Head around the corner from the equestrian school to the Sandeman Bodega, walk through the patio and into the building to reach the visitor reception area. Make your reservation for an English tour by calling 956-30-1100. English is spoken on the phone. 2004 prices: €4.50. (Allow 1+ hours, including a leisurely tasting)

Food tip: You will probably be in the area around lunchtime. Try Bar Los Cisnes located on Calle Divina Pastora. The house specialty, *solomillo al oloroso viejo* (pork tenderloin in a sweet sherry sauce), is *muy delicioso*! After walking out of the Equestrian School's gates, turn right, cross the street, and turn left onto Calle Divina Pastora. The café will be on the left hand side of the street, about half a block down.

Highlight: Watching the very proud, dancing, prancing, trotting, kicking horses as they practiced their steps to a background of flamenco guitar music.

Lowlight: Rushing through lunch with a squirmy baby trying to make a 14:00 bodega tour, and then finding out the 14:00 tour was actually scheduled for 14:30! Double-check your time when you make your reservation.

Sidelight: Visit the nearly deserted Museo del Enganche (Carriage Museum) to see antique carriages and their well-stocked horse stables. The Museo del Enganche is associated with the equestrian school. Pay one euro more when you buy your equestrian school ticket to include entry into this museum. It's located directly across the street from the Sandeman Bodega entrance on Calle Pizarro. (Allow one hour depending on what catches your fancy.)

Hint: Probably the most limiting factor of the day is the time the Equestrian school closes. On practice days it closes at 13:00, so you probably want to plan to see this first.

Directions: From Rota, take the A-491 to the N-IV north to Jerez. Pass by the city center exit and the exit for the hospital. At the next traffic circle (Bodegas Garvey buildings on your left) enter the traffic circle and take the 4:00 exit onto Avenida Tomás García Figueras. At the second stoplight, turn right onto Avenida Duque de Abrantes (signs point toward the equestrian school). In 0.2 miles (0.3 km) you will pass the school on your right. Continue down the street, as there is no parking here. Turn right at the next street, Calle Pizarro. The Sandeman Bodega will be on your right. Look for street parking here, or take a right or left onto Calle Fernando de la Cuedra to find residential street parking.

Jerez is also easily accessible by train. From the El Puerto de Santa María train station, travel one stop (10 minutes) to the Jerez station and catch a quick taxi to the equestrian school. Check out www.renfe.es/ingles for timetables.

Jerez Travel Notes:

Laguna de Medina

Laguna de Medina, located southeast of Jerez off the A-381, is a large lagoon featuring bird-life, a marshy eco-system, and a dirt path bordering the lagoon. If traveling with little ones, it should be possible to use a jogging stroller during the dry months. While certainly not overly challenging for a hike, it is a quick trip to get out, breathe some fresh air, and see a little nature.

Travel time: About 23 minutes.

Things to do in a day:

- ❑ Hike next to the lagoon for a little nature experience. The trailhead map reads, "1.4 km, 30 minutes, easy hike." Follow the trail in one-direction and when you get to the end, turn around and come back. (Allow one hour total)

- ❑ Look for birds migrating on the European-North African circuit.

Food tip: Have a bite to eat at home, bring a bottle of water, and you're all set.

Highlight: Nature hiking 23 minutes from the base!

Lowlight: Ankle deep mud and an impassable flooded trail in the month of December.

Sidelight: On your way to and from Laguna de Medina, you will pass La Cartuja, a former Carthusian monastery. This impressive building has a beautiful entryway with a courtyard and church within. The elaborate façade on the church dates from the 17th century, but the church itself is older. While the main gate on the driveway is normally closed, there is a small gate to the right set in the wall that will be open. Park here, but don't block the driveway. Spend 15 minutes poking around this cool piece of history.

Hint: The local park ranger said that April, May, and October are some of the better months to visit Laguna de Medina. In April, we saw water birds, frogs, wildflowers, and some exotic-looking insects.

Directions: From Rota, drive towards Jerez on the A-491. At the casino/water park traffic circle take the 2:00 exit towards El Portal (CA-201). In six miles (10 km), when the road comes to a 'T' at a traffic circle, turn right onto the A-381. Follow this road for 3.5 miles (5.6 km) and turn left at the crossroad with the sign that leads to Laguna de Medina. Follow this smaller road for about 0.6 miles (one km). There will be a little sign that reads Laguna de Medina and dirt parking will be just off the street on your right. The trailhead to the lagoon will be across the street on your left. During 2004 road construction projects, you may be detoured past the entrance to the lagoon without having to make the left-hand turn.

To get to the Carthusian monastery from Rota, after you turn right at the 'T' intersection onto the A-381, travel about 0.3 miles (0.5 km) and it will be on your right.

Laguna de Medina Travel Notes:

La Rábida

History buffs, this is the day trip for you! La Rábida, just outside Huelva, is rich in Christopher Columbus history. You can visit the monastery where he stayed while petitioning Queen Isabel for support, and then explore floating replicas of the Niña, Pinta, and Santa María. All the sites are grouped together, so a visit to La Rábida makes for an easy trip, and the historical significance makes for a meaningful one.

Travel time: About two hours 25 minutes.

Things to do in a day:

❑ Wander through the monastery where Christopher Columbus stayed. See the chapel where he prayed before departing on his voyage to the New World, and be inspired by the tiny room called "The

Cradle of America" where he revealed his plans and dreams to the resident friars. Attractive gardens front the monastery. www. monateriodelarabida.com. Open in the morning from 10:00–13:00 on Monday–Saturday, and from 10:45–13:00 on Sunday. Open in the afternoon from 16:00–18:15 in the winter, from 16:00–19:00 in the summer, and from 16:00–20:00 in August. 2004 prices: €2.50, €3 with an audio-guide, and €6 for families. (Allow one hour)

❑ Scamper aboard full-size replicas of the Niña, Pinta, and Santa María at the Muelle de las Carabelas (Wharf of the Caravels—by definition, a caravel is a ship from the 15th and 16th centuries with a broad bow, high narrow poop deck, and usually three masts). You'll be surprised at the small size of these trans-Atlantic vessels. There is a small museum in the building in front of the ships. Open April–September on Tuesday–Friday from 10:00–14:00 and 17:00–21:00, and Saturday and Sunday from 11:00–20:00. Open September–April on Tuesday–Sunday from 10:00–19:00. Closed Monday. 2004 prices: €3, €6.25 for families, and children under 5 free. (Allow 30–60 minutes)

❑ Stop at the José Celestino Mutis Botanical Park. There are waterscapes and walking paths that wind around a wide variety of plants and flowers. Open April–September on Tuesday–Friday from 10:00–14:00 and 17:00–21:00, and Saturday and Sunday from 11:00–20:00. Open September–April on Tuesday–Sunday from 10:00–19:00. Closed Monday. 2004 prices: €1.50, families €3, and children under 5 free. (Allow 30+ minutes)

Food tip: If you need a bite to eat, there is a convenient bar serving *tapas* and rations at Muella de las Carabelas, where the ships are docked. There is also a *venta* restaurant next door to the monastery, but based on our experience, it closes about the same time the monastery visiting hours are over.

Highlight: Walking through the monastery where Christopher Columbus lived, prayed, and thought big thoughts over 500 years ago.

Lowlight: Negotiating Huelva's downtown streets in sheeting rain without a map. (We were attempting to find Huelva's Tourist Information Office, but eventually gave up.)

Sidelight: Only a few miles from La Rábida lies Huelva, a big city that never seems to get much of a write-up in travel books. On a brief drive through the downtown area we saw big city shopping, interesting architecture, and impressive fountains. If you leave for La Rábida early enough in the morning, you may have time to explore Huelva on your own.

Hint: Be wary of traveling past Sevilla on a weekday at the start of siesta, especially in inclement weather. If you do, prepare yourself for big-city traffic and long delays.

Directions: From Rota, drive towards Jerez on the A-491. At the casino/water park traffic circle take the 2:00 exit towards El Portal (CA-201). In six miles (10 km), when the road comes to a 'T' at a traffic circle, turn right onto the A-381. In one mile (1.6 km), take the A-4 north to Sevilla, and when you reach Sevilla, take the E-1/A-49 towards Huelva and Portugal. Stay on the E-1/A-49 for about 48 miles (77 km). Take the left lane exit to Huelva on the H-31. After about four miles (six km), exit towards La Rábida on the H-30/N-442. The La Rábida exit is located before you reach Huelva's city center, effectively bypassing Huelva. Drive about 6.5 miles (10 km) on the H-30/N-442 and when you reach a traffic circle with signs pointing to La Rábida, take the 9:00 exit. In 0.4 miles (0.6 km) turn left to La Rábida.

The botanical gardens are located in the first dirt parking lot immediately to the right. Traveling further down this road about 0.3 miles (0.5 km) brings you to a traffic circle. Turn right to get the monastery. Signs read "Universidad International de Andalucía." The monastery will be on your left in about 0.2 miles (0.3 km). To get to the ships and museum, retrace your steps to the traffic circle and take the right exit and drive about 0.1 miles (0.1 km) continuing down the road you were on. Turn right at the next traffic circle and the museum will be on your left in about 0.2 miles (0.3 km). Enter the museum building to reach the ships.

La Rábida Travel Notes:

Marbella

Visit Marbella and neighboring Puerto Banús to catch a glimpse of how the jet set lives. Marbella is considered a playground for the rich and famous—a place to dock their yachts and spend their wealth at Cartier, Bulgari, Hermes, and Salvatore Ferragamo. Do you need that kind of money to enjoy Marbella? Not if you're content with the sparkling Mediterranean, a quaint old town, and window-shopping. Oh, well the parking costs a bit more than average!

Travel time: About two hours 10 minutes.

Things to do in a day:

- ❑ Wander through the Parque de la Constitución. It's a pretty park and a convenient place to stretch your legs and let the kids run. The Tourist Information Office is located just outside the park towards the beach. The office is open on Monday–Friday from 9:30–21:00, and Saturday from 10:00–14:00.

- ❑ Head to the beach and walk along the beach path. If you've never done it before, stick your feet in the Mediterranean just to say that you have. Stroll eastward and pass little shops and stands selling everything from bathing suits to paintings to belly dancing outfits.

- ❑ Walk past sculptures and fountains on Avenida del Mar on your way to the old town. Explore the narrow cobblestone streets and buildings in the old part of town. Enjoy a cool drink shaded by orange trees and umbrellas in the delightful Plaza de los Naranjos (Orange Tree Plaza).

- ❑ Walk back to your car and drive to Puerto Banús.

- ❑ Head to the harbor and gawk at the ostentatious yachts docked at Puerto Banús.

❑ Wander through the expensive Puerto Banús shopping district—everywhere you look there seems to be an expensive shopping district. There are many stores on the street bordering the harbor, and more inland. Watch boys, young and old, get their pictures taken next to expensive cars.

Food tip: American commercialism has reached Marbella, and if you've lived a while in Spain without your favorite chain restaurant, you'll be glad to hear it. Tony Roma's can be found on your drive from Marbella to Puerto Banús on the right side of the stretch of road called "The Golden Mile." Trader Vic's can be found on your left in the La Alcazaba complex just before entering central Puerto Banús. TGIFriday's can be found in the heart of Puerto Banús within the outdoor commercial center of Marina Banús. Enjoy your taste of America!

Highlight: The Plaza de los Naranjos. Marbella offers a lot of glitz, but the charm of the city lies in this plaza at the heart of the old town.

Lowlight: Yikes! We paid a lot of money for parking!

Sidelight: If you have some extra time and a wild animal park is more your style, consider visiting Selwo Aventura located between Marbella and Estepona at the 162.5 kilometer exit on the N-340. The animals roam in a large wild territory and the park offers adventure activities as well. You can even stay overnight in the Watu or Masai Villages. The park is open daily from 10:00–18:00. 2004 prices: €19.50 for adults, €14 for children 4–12, and free for children three-and-under. An overnight stay is €37 for adults, €18.50 for children 4–12, and free for children three-and-under (add an additional fee of €6 during high season). You can find out more information on the web at www.selwo.es.

Hint: If you choose to eat at a Spanish beachside restaurant with great views and only mediocre food, and there happens to be a wedding party waiting for the neighboring restaurant to open up, don't expect a quiet meal. What you *should* expect is for some member of the wedding party to be out on the beach lighting off cherry bombs and scaring the daylights out of anyone within earshot.

Directions: Take the inland route to save time. From Rota, drive towards Jerez on the A-491, and at the casino/water park traffic circle take the 2:00 exit towards El Portal (CA-201). In six miles (10 km), when the road comes to a 'T' at a traffic circle, turn right onto the A-381. Travel on this road for about 54 miles (87 km), passing Los Barrios, until the road intersects with the A-7/E-15. Turn east towards Gibraltar, Malaga, and San Roque. In about 14 miles (22 km) you will make the decision whether to stay on the A-7/E-15 toll road or take the free coastal road. On the toll road, there were two tolls totaling €6.05 (2004 prices) and, without any traffic delays, a total time savings of about 15 minutes by avoiding numerous traffic circles.

To get into downtown Marbella, consider consulting an Internet site for maps and directions, or you can follow the sketchy route we took. Take the second Marbella exit, exit 185, towards Marbella. At the first traffic circle, turn right onto Avenida Duque de Lema. Follow the road straight until it ends near the water. Turn right onto Avenida de Severo Ochoa, following signs towards the old town. Pass the pedestrian street leading to the Plaza de los Naranjos on your right, and the park-like Paseo de la Alameda on your left. In a few blocks turn left at the light onto Avenida Arias Maldonado, following signs to the Tourist Information Office. There will be an underground parking garage in a few blocks on your right, across the street from the Parque de la Constitución.

To reach Puerto Banús, head back to the main road paralleling the water, now called Avenida Ricardo, and drive west. This road is also called "The Golden Mile." Drive on this road until you reach the turnoff to Puerto Banús. Head towards the harbor and the downtown area. When you reach the beach, turn right and look for a parking garage. There's a very expensive one immediately to your right, but I think there may be cheaper ones if you park in one of the commercial centers' garages. Walk from your car to the harbor.

Marbella Travel Notes:

1. PARQUE DE LA CONSTITUCIÓN 4. AVENIDA DEL MAR
2. TOURISM OFFICE   5. PASEO DE LA ALAMEDA
3. BEACH WALK   6. PLAZA DE LOS NARANJOS

TO
PUERTO BANÚS

NOT TO SCALE

TO
AUTOVIA

MEDITERRANEAN SEA

MARBELLA

JRR
2004

Medina Sidonia

Medina Sidonia is a small village located along the "route of the bull," an area in Andalucía known for prime bull raising pastures. The town can claim Phoenician, Roman, Visigoth, and Moorish roots. Sitting on top of a hill 300 meters high, it has lovely vistas of the Bay of Cádiz and the surrounding agricultural fields. But let's be honest, the real reason to visit Medina Sidonia can be summed up in one word…dessert.

Travel time: Approximately 50 minutes.

Things to do in a day:

- ❑ Start at the Plaza de España to find restaurants, a pastry shop, and the *ayuntamiento* (the town hall).

- ❑ Pop into the church, Iglesia de la Victoria, for a quick visit if it's open.

- ❑ Walk uphill to the Iglesia de Santa María la Mayor. Climb the narrow and slightly claustrophobic circular staircase to the top of the bell tower for fabulous views. Walk through and admire the interior of the church. Open from 10:30–14:00 and 16:00–18:30. 2003 prices: €2. (Allow 30 minutes for the bell tower and 30 minutes for the church)

- ❑ Hike up to the castle ruins. They're mostly rubble, but there's a nice view of the church and town. (Allow 30 minutes)

- ❑ Walk to the Moorish arch, Arco de la Pastora, for a nice photo opportunity.

Food tip: In the Plaza de España, try Bar Cádiz Restaurante. Located on the main plaza (Plaza de España 13) it has a pretty, vine-covered, interior patio and serves good stews, brochettes (meat and vegetables grilled on a skewer), and lots of local specialties.

Highlight: A toss-up between great vistas from the very top of the church bell tower and being pulled in off the street by a local gentleman at the *ayuntamiento* to be offered free hot chocolate and an almond-flavored donut four days before Christmas.

Lowlight: A cold, bracing December wind on top of that church bell tower.

Sidelight: Medina Sidonia is considered the cake and pastry capital of the province of Cádiz, and if you see and taste their product, you'll know why. The *alfajor* is the most typical cake from Medina and reportedly the recipe has been handed down for generations. Also not to be missed are the *polvorones*, delicious crumbly shortbread. One centrally located pastry shop is Sobrina de las Trejas, located at Plaza de España 7. It was founded in 1852, so you know it's authentic. Bring extra euro…we walked out of the shop with a kilo of pastries by the time we were done!

Hints:

1. If you don't feel like walking up the hill to the Iglesia de Santa María, there is a plaza in front of the church with parking.

2. Check out www.medinasidonia.com for some photographs and an interactive map before your trip.

Directions: From Rota, drive towards Jerez on the A-491. At the casino/water park traffic circle take the 2:00 exit towards El Portal (CA-201). In six miles (10 km), when the road comes to a 'T' at a traffic circle, turn right onto the A-381. Follow this road 17 miles (27 km) then exit to the right towards Medina Sidonia. On the outskirts of the city bear left at the Roman-looking fountain and follow signs to the city center, winding your way through the streets (right then left, right then left). You will reach a large plaza, the Plaza de España. Follow the road past the plaza to find a small dirt parking area to the right.

Medina Sidonia Travel Notes:

MEDINA SIDONIA

NOT TO SCALE

JEREZ

1. ARCO DE LA PASTORA
2. IGLESIA DE LA VICTORIA
3. PLAZA DE ESPAÑA
4. AYUNTAMIENTO (CITY HALL)
5. TOURISM OFFICE
6. IGLESIA DE STE MARÍA
7. CASTILLO (CASTLE)

Olvera

Olvera is a delightful *pueblo blanco* (white village) that draws travelers willing to detour off the beaten path. Most of the brilliant whitewashed town looks up to the huge church placed squarely near the top of a hill. Next door to the church, the old fortress castle still seems to be guarding the town on its precariously balanced, rocky perch. Olvera's charms are waiting to be discovered. Quick! Go before they are!

Travel time: About one hour 40 minutes.

Things to do in a day:

❑ Explore the old fortress castle. The entrance is located off the Plaza de la Iglesia. The castle was closed in mid-2004 for restorations but was due to open at the end of the year. Photos show narrow circular staircases to climb and a bird's eye view of the surrounding countryside. Open in the winter on Tuesday–Sunday from 10:30–14:00 and 16:00–18:00. Open in the summer on Tuesday–Sunday from 10:30–14:00 and 16:00–19:00.

❑   Visit the city museum, also located off the Plaza de la Iglesia, which is open the same hours as the castle. While light on artifacts, €1.20 (2004 prices) will get you displays and nice photos on the history of Olvera. (Allow 15 minutes)

❑   See the Monumento al Sagrado Corazón (Sacred Heart Monument). The entrance is located off the Plaza de Andalucía. Walk past the waterfall fountain, up the stairs to the little bird aviary, and continue to the top where a towering statue of Jesus looks upon the town. Open in the winter from 10:00–14:00 and 16:00–18:00. Open in the summer from 10:30–13:30 and 18:00–20:00. (Allow 30+ minutes)

❑   Walk through the open market if you arrive on a Saturday. The market is located on the main street entering town. It operates from about 10:00–14:00 on Saturday.

Food tip: Try Bar Pepe Rayas located in the Plaza del Ayuntamiento. Sit outdoors for excellent views of the church and castle. This is the place to load up on some fairly inexpensive *tapas*. The *rolito de pollo* (deep-fried chicken stuffed with spinach), *patatas rellenas* (deep-fried potato croquettes stuffed with tuna), *corrillada en salsa* (tender pork in sauce), *brocheta del pollo* (chicken kebob), *calamares fritas* (deep fried calamari rings and tentacles), *queso de la sierra* (local cheese), and *pimientos del piquello* (deep-fried red peppers stuffed with tuna, eggs, and breadcrumbs) are all highly recommended—especially since most came with a delicious, marinated potato salad. The only one I wouldn't order again is the Andalucían specialty *rabo del toro* (oxtail). I had to try it once since it was known as a specialty, but decided I really didn't enjoy trying to pick meat off something that looked like the bony cross-section of an animal's vertebrae.

Highlight: Discovering and exploring this quaint little town on our fortieth day trip.

Lowlight: The towering castle we had often admired from the road during other travels was closed for restorations.

Sidelight: Before you leave town, check out the Vía Verde de la Sierra (Green Track of the Sierra) that starts in Olvera. It's located about 0.5 miles (0.8 km) downhill from the bus station. The Vía Verde is a 36-kilometer trail between Olvera and Puerto Serrano that follows old railroad tracks and is traveled by foot, bike, or horseback. The track goes through 30 train tunnels, passes by five old railway stations, and for part of the way borders the Río Guadalete (Guadalete River). Three of the old railway stations have been converted into hotels with restaurants.

For a weekend adventure, try parking in Puerto Serrano and biking to Olvera, an elevation gain of 250 meters. Stay the night in Olvera's railway station hotel, Hotel Estación Verde (661-46-3207). Cruise back to Puerto Serrano the next day. If your Spanish is good, try www.fundacionviaverdedelasierra.com for more information. If you don't have a bike, you should be able to rent one there (or if you're military, try the Outdoor Recreation Center at Naval Base Rota).

Hint: If you wake up late on a Saturday but still want to do a day trip, Olvera may be your perfect choice. This is one of the few towns where tourist attractions are open late afternoon on the weekends.

Directions: From Rota, drive towards Jerez on the A-491. At the casino/water park traffic circle take the 2:00 exit towards El Portal (CA-201). In six miles (10 km), when the road comes to a 'T' at a traffic circle, turn right onto the A-381. In one mile (1.6 km), take the A-4 north to Sevilla. In three miles (five km), take the A-382 exit. Turn right towards Arcos de la Frontera. Follow the A-382 for about 55 miles (89 km) and take the left turn to Olvera on the CA-0447. Follow this road about 1.5 miles (2.4 km). You will see the castle on your right. Park anywhere on this main street. Parking may be a little crowded on Saturday mornings due to the street market, so you may have to walk a little. Once on foot, follow the uphill roads to reach the castle.

Olvera Travel Notes:

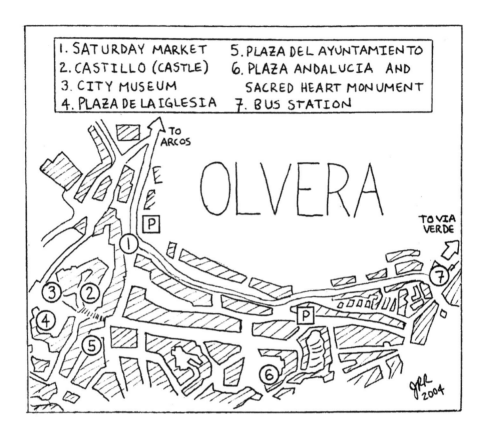

1. SATURDAY MARKET
2. CASTILLO (CASTLE)
3. CITY MUSEUM
4. PLAZA DE LA IGLESIA
5. PLAZA DEL AYUNTAMIENTO
6. PLAZA ANDALUCIA AND
   SACRED HEART MONUMENT
7. BUS STATION

Ronda

Ronda seems to be everyone's favorite city for a number of reasons: history, architecture, shopping, vistas, and menus in English. While Ronda gets its share of tourists, the city maintains its charm despite the crowds. Make some time to spend a day or two here enjoying the beauty of this city and you'll agree.

Travel time: About two hours.

Things to do:

❑   Play matador (or bull) in the center of the bullring. This bullring is claimed to be the oldest in Spain. There's an attached museum to visit and learn about the history of modern bullfighting. www.rmcr.org. Open daily November–February from 10:00–18:00;

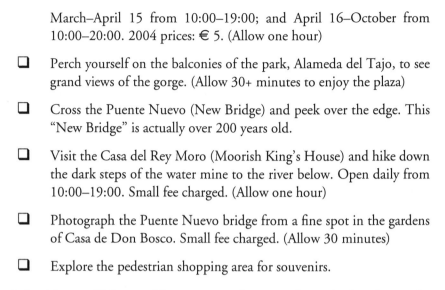

March–April 15 from 10:00–19:00; and April 16–October from 10:00–20:00. 2004 prices: € 5. (Allow one hour)

❑ Perch yourself on the balconies of the park, Alameda del Tajo, to see grand views of the gorge. (Allow 30+ minutes to enjoy the plaza)

❑ Cross the Puente Nuevo (New Bridge) and peek over the edge. This "New Bridge" is actually over 200 years old.

❑ Visit the Casa del Rey Moro (Moorish King's House) and hike down the dark steps of the water mine to the river below. Open daily from 10:00–19:00. Small fee charged. (Allow one hour)

❑ Photograph the Puente Nuevo bridge from a fine spot in the gardens of Casa de Don Bosco. Small fee charged. (Allow 30 minutes)

❑ Explore the pedestrian shopping area for souvenirs.

Food tip: Next to El Puente Nuevo, across the street from the Parador, is the Hotel-Restaurante Don Migel located at Plaza de España 4&5. Make your way down the stairs to the cafeteria and enjoy a cold drink on the balcony. There are up-close views of the bridge and river gorge. It oozes with atmosphere.

Highlight: Finding sensational views of the bridge from a deserted balcony with a cold beer in hand (see food tip).

Lowlight: After dropping one tire off an 18-inch cobblestone ledge while trying to park on city streets, a little girl threw rocks at our car.

Sidelight: After crossing El Puente Nuevo, turn right onto the cobblestone street and walk to the Plaza del Campillo. There is a trailhead here leading into the gorge. Hike partway down to the ruins of Albacara, walls from the Moorish period, for a prime photo opportunity of the bridge.

Hints:

1. If staying overnight in Ronda, be aware there are *many* hotels in Ronda, not just the two or three listed in all the guidebooks. Shop around.

2. If staying overnight near the city center, bring earplugs or background music. Not even double-paned windows will eliminate the sounds of the 2 a.m. revelers.

3. There is a helpful information office with maps of the city in the plaza next to the bullring.

4. If you are looking for a grassy area for a baby to crawl, head towards the Paseo Blas Infante.

Directions: From Rota, drive towards Jerez on the A-491. At the casino/water park traffic circle take the 2:00 exit towards El Portal (CA-201). In six miles (10 km), when the road comes to a 'T' at a traffic circle, turn right onto the A-381. In one mile (1.6 km), take the A-4 north to Sevilla. In three miles (five km), take the A-382 exit. Turn right towards Arcos de la Frontera. Follow the A-382 for about 47 miles (76 km). Turn onto the A-376, signs point towards Ronda. Travel the A-376 about 10 miles (16 km) and there will be a right hand turn with signs pointing to the Parador and Ronda. Follow the "centro urbana" and "centro ciudad" signs into town. In one mile (1.6 km), when Jerez Street becomes Virgen de la Paz, there will be an underground parking garage to the right, across from the Hotel Royal and next to the Iglesia de la Merced church. If this parking lot is full, follow parking signs to other lots in the city, but be advised that the "Multi-cine" parking lot is not very close to the city center.

Ronda Travel Notes:

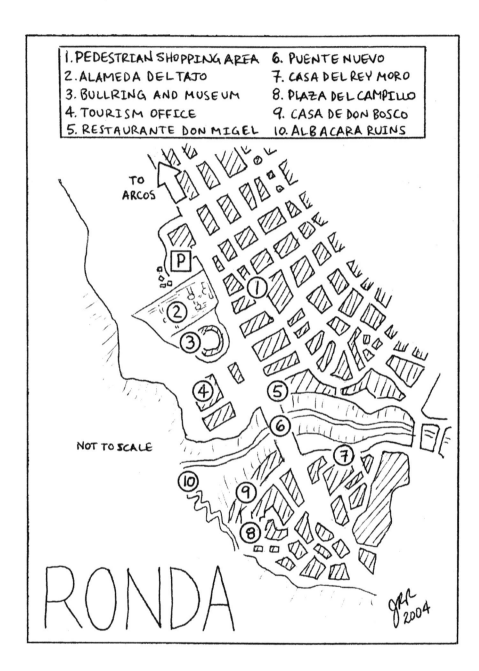

1. PEDESTRIAN SHOPPING AREA
2. ALAMEDA DEL TAJO
3. BULLRING AND MUSEUM
4. TOURISM OFFICE
5. RESTAURANTE DON MIGEL
6. PUENTE NUEVO
7. CASA DEL REY MORO
8. PLAZA DEL CAMPILLO
9. CASA DE DON BOSCO
10. ALBACARA RUINS

TO ARCOS

NOT TO SCALE

RONDA

JRR 2004

Rota

All right, so today isn't so much a day trip *from* Rota, as a day trip *in* Rota, but if you need a suggestion on what to do that's easy and local when your friends and relatives visit, read on. If you're in the military, it's a little something to do with that family you're sponsoring after they arrive. Conveniently, this day trip can be done almost any time of year and almost any time of day, including the afternoon siesta hours. This quick trip into Rota may be the perfect introduction to Spain and a nice way to walk off some jet lag.

Travel time: About six minutes.

Things to do in a day:

☐   Walk from the marina along the water, around the Hotel Duque along the boardwalk, and through the arch in the wall to the Bartolomé Perez Plaza to see the cathedral and castle. (Allow five minutes to walk to the plaza)

❑   Admire the cathedral, Parroquia Nuestra Señora de la O, and if you're there between 9:00–13:00 or 18:30–21:00, go in for a visit. Free. (Allow 15 minutes)

❑   Climb the short flight of stairs to enter the castle, Castillo de Luna. Narrow columns and arches surround the interior courtyard, which has a small central fountain and wooden benches you can relax on and breathe in the atmosphere. Free. (Allow 15 minutes)

❑   Walk up the pedestrian streets, Charco and García Sánchez, and do some window-shopping. (Allow 20+ minutes)

❑   Walk back down to the beach path and continue to follow it to its end. (Allow 10 minutes)

❑   Stroll through the Parque Atlantico. Turn right up the last street on the beach path, A. Santiago Guillén Moreno, to reach the entrance on your left. There are picnic tables, grassy areas, playground equipment, and (if you are two years old) pigeons to chase. (Allow five minutes to one hour depending on whom you're traveling with.)

❑   Walk back along the beach path to your car. Listen to the sound of the surf while ignoring any overly loud music blaring from apartments. (Allow 25–30 minutes)

Food tip: There are numerous cafes lining the beachfront serving drinks, *tapas*, and individual paella portions. There's also a Kentucky Fried Chicken located midway down the beach path at the corner of the Plaza de Jesús Nazareno. With towering panoramic windows overlooking the sparkling Atlantic, it has to be one of the best-located KFC's in the world.

Highlight: The castle courtyard. It's like a beautiful oasis in the heart of Rota.

Lowlight: Attempting to walk to the Botanical Gardens shown at the far edge of Rota's tourist map. Notice these gardens are not listed in the "Things to do" section. After walking for about 20 minutes from the Parque Atlantico towards the gardens, we decided "Enough!" and turned around. We think the gardens were further away than what our map scale indicated.

Sidelight: If you are visiting on a summer weekend, swing by the cathedral in the early evening. Summer is the season for weddings, and the Rota cathedral is the place to see them. On busy weekends there may be multiple weddings happening, one after another. If you linger in the plaza with a cold drink you may get to see beautiful brides, traditionally-dressed Spanish women with lace *mantillas* in their hair (delicate lace draped over a large decorative comb), and fancy cars lined up to whisk the happy couple away. We were lucky enough to see a flamenco finale to a summer wedding. As the bride and groom departed the church, a flamenco guitarist played and the couple broke into dance while all the guests clapped in rhythm. What a fabulous way to enjoy the culture of Spain on a warm summer evening!

Hint: Don't forget the sunscreen. You can get a sunburn even on overcast days.

Directions: From the Naval Base's Rota gate, drive straight and at the first traffic circle go 3/4 of the way around the circle to continue on Calvario, the cobblestone street. At 0.4 miles (0.6 km) bear left on Veracruz. At 0.5 miles (0.8 km) from the base, go around the traffic circle, take the 11:00 exit, and drive along the shoreline. At 0.7 miles (1.1 km) from the base go around the traffic circle, take the 9:00 exit, and enter the marina parking lot. During summer you will have to pay for parking, but the rest of the year it should be free. Walk towards the lighthouse and you will see the beginning of the Rota beach boardwalk. The archway leading to the castle and church is a few yards down the boardwalk.

Rota Travel Notes:

1. MARINA ENTRANCE   4. CASTILLO DE LUNA
2. ARCH (HOTEL DUQUE) 5. PEDESTRIAN STREET
3. CATHEDRAL   6. KENTUCKY FRIED CHICKEN

ROTA

NOT TO SCALE

TO NB ROTA

P

AVENIDA SAN FERNANDO

WALK ROUTE

5

5

3

4

6

TO PARQUE ATLANTICO

BOARDWALK

2

ATLANTIC OCEAN

1

jm 2004

Sanlúcar de Barrameda

Historical Sanlúcar is a gem. This sleepy little waterside town has a wealth of historical buildings to be discovered and explored. Many of the buildings are currently in use by the city, so it's no problem to go in and ask to take a look around. As they are city buildings, Monday through Friday mornings are probably the best times to visit.

Travel time: About 35 minutes.

Things to do in a day:

❑ Step up from the parking garage onto the walking avenue, Alzada del Ejercito. Visit the Tourist Information Office located here for a map of the city. The Information Office is open from 10:00–14:00 and 16:00–18:00 (winter hours).

❑ Explore the old town and walk into the open historical buildings. In a two hour walk you should be able to see the Plaza del Cabildo; the old city hall (now a library); the exterior of the churches Trinidad, Los Desamparados, and Nuestra Señora de la O; the auditorium La Merced; Las Covachas; the patio of the current town hall in the Palace of Orleáns and Bourbón; the gardens of the Palace of Medina Sidonia; and the exterior of the Santiago Castle.

❑ Visit the Barbadillo Museum (Calle Sevilla 1) to learn about Manzanilla sherry or to simply purchase some sherry and glasses. The museum, only open as a guided tour, is open on Monday–Saturday from 11:00–15:00; however, tours in English are currently only offered at 11:00. 2004 prices: €3. Telephone: 956-38-5500. www.barbadillo.com

Food tips: There are a few things for which Sanlúcar is renown: Manzanilla sherry, *gambas* (prawns) and *langostinos* (king prawns). The Manzanilla sherry is light in color and dry due to the *flor* present year round during the aging process. . The local seafood is delicious, but forewarned is forearmed—most *gambas* and *langostinos* come looking like they just swam in from the bay. If you'd rather not have the eyes of your lunch looking back at you, you might try *gambas al ajillo* (prawns with garlic).

There are plenty of bars and cafés in the main square, Plaza del Cabildo. The waterside restaurants near the marina and ferry landings are really too far to walk just for a meal.

Highlight: Being surprised by the uniqueness of our neighboring town, Sanlúcar. There were numerous, beautiful buildings with open access, each with descriptive signs posted in English and Spanish.

Lowlight: Bad timing. We found a very cute children's chair while window-shopping but we couldn't get back to the shop before they closed for siesta. We also discovered that the Barbadillo Museum was only open for English tours at 11:00—we weren't even out of the house by then.

Sidelight: In August, Sanlúcar is best known for its beachside horse races. This sensational event is actually part of the professional racing circuit, not just a promotional gimmick dreamed up by the city's tourism office. Unfortunately, there are not any hard and fast dates when the races occur. The schedule and start times naturally depend on the tides!

So, speaking as generally as possible, races are held two weekends (Friday, Saturday, and Sunday) in early August, but not necessarily on consecutive weekends. They take place in the early evening when the tide is low. There are between three and six races a night—ours started around 18:00 with about half an hour between races. The racecourse is about a mile long stretch of beach, so getting a good viewing spot shouldn't be a problem.

Your suggested itinerary is: watch the horses parade down the beach for the upcoming race, place a small bet (pocket change) with one of the enterprising kids at any number of "betting booths", jockey for the best viewing position at the barricade as the police summon everyone from the water, prepare yourself as the police vehicle comes screaming by the waiting crowds, cheer like mad as the horses come thundering past, hop the barricade so you can watch the finish much further down the beach, pocket your losing ticket, and go stick your feet in the water while you wait for the next race.

What we learned (the hard way) is to plan the outing like you are spending the day at the beach. Bring beach towels, cold drinks, snacks, sunscreen(!), and anything else you might need on a multiple-hour trip to the beach. Parking was easy along Avenida V Centenario, follow signs to the beach, but it is a good idea to park in the "out" direction so you don't get stuck trying to turn around at traffic circles and stoplights with the rest of the masses.

This is a really unique and spectacular event. If you hear the horse races are upcoming, make every effort to go!

Hint: At the Barbadillo Museum shop there is a book of Spanish poems written by Manuel Barbadillo Rodríguez, *Poemas a Sanlúcar.* He writes about Sanlúcar, the sea, and Manzanilla. The book does double duty, it makes for a unique Sanlúcar souvenir and it can be used as an interesting tool for practicing your Spanish.

Directions: From Naval Base Rota, exit the Rota gate and take an immediate right onto the CA-603. Drive three miles (five km) and get onto the A-491 towards Chipiona. Drive approximately three miles (five km) and turn right following signs to Sanlúcar de Barrameda. Drive six miles (10 km) and turn right at the stop sign. Drive one mile (1.6 km) to reach a large traffic circle with a McDonalds. Take the 9:00 exit towards the beaches. In about 0.6 miles (one km) at the traffic circle, take the 3:00 exit towards the Tourist Information Office and the "centro urbano". In 0.2 miles (0.3 km) you will reach the large plaza, Alzada del Ejercito, and find an underground parking garage directly in front of you.

From El Puerto de Santa María, it is quicker to go to Sanlúcar via the CA-602. Take the A-491 to the El Puerto/Sanlúcar exit and turn left onto the CA-602 towards Sanlúcar. Follow this road 12 miles (19 km) and you will enter Sanlúcar. At the traffic light turn left, following signs to the beaches and city center. In about 0.7 miles (1.1 km) at the large traffic circle with the McDonalds take the 3:00 exit towards the beaches. In about 0.6 miles (one km) at the traffic circle, take the 3:00 exit towards the Tourist Information Office and the "centro urbano". In 0.2 miles (0.3 km) you will reach the large plaza, Alzada del Ejercito, and find an underground parking garage directly in front of you.

Sanlúcar de Barrameda Travel Notes:

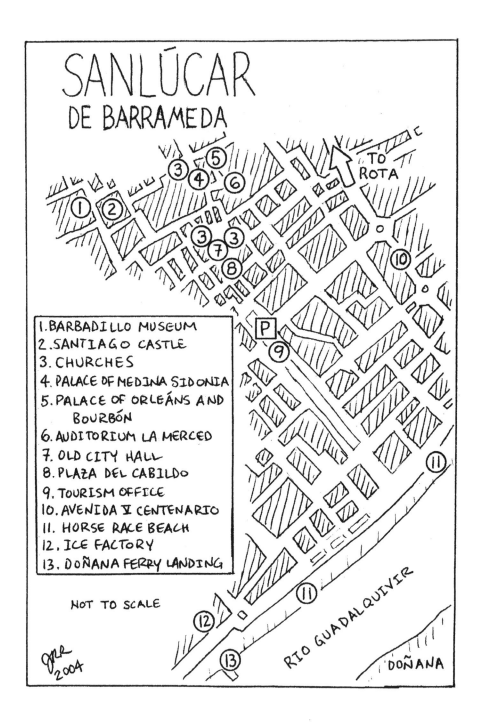

SANLÚCAR
DE BARRAMEDA

TO ROTA

1. BARBADILLO MUSEUM
2. SANTIAGO CASTLE
3. CHURCHES
4. PALACE OF MEDINA SIDONIA
5. PALACE OF ORLEÁNS AND
   BOURBÓN
6. AUDITORIUM LA MERCED
7. OLD CITY HALL
8. PLAZA DEL CABILDO
9. TOURISM OFFICE
10. AVENIDA V CENTENARIO
11. HORSE RACE BEACH
12. ICE FACTORY
13. DOÑANA FERRY LANDING

NOT TO SCALE

RIO GUADALQUIVIR

DOÑANA

2004

Sevilla I

Sevilla is a big city with big-ticket tourist sites, a "must-see" city on most people's itineraries. If you have only one day in Sevilla, certainly see the Cathedral and its tower La Giralda, the Royal Palace (see Sevilla II), and anything else you can squeeze into your day. But if you live in the region, this city deserves more than a one-day trip. Come back for extra servings!

Travel time: By train, from the El Puerto de Santa María station to the Sevilla-Santa Justa station, one hour 10 minutes to one hour 20 minutes depending on your train, plus a 15-minute taxi ride or 45-minute walk into the center of town. If driving, it takes about one hour 20 minutes.

Things to do in a day:

- ❑ Wander through the Cathedral and be amazed at its sheer size and beauty. Open on Monday–Saturday from 11:00–17:00, and Sunday from 1400–1600. 2004 prices: €7, free for children under 12, €3 for an audio-guide. Sundays free. (Allow 30 minutes)

- ❑ Hike up La Giralda's 34 ramps to get a bird's eye view of the city. This is feasible with a stroller, but you will exert some energy. There are steps near the very top, so you'll have to park the stroller at the base of the steps. (Allow 30+ minutes)

- ❑ Take a breather away from tourists in a small and secluded plaza. Plaza de Santa Marta is located near the cathedral on the corner of the Plaza Virgen de los Reyes. The small street looks like a back alley but ends around the corner at a quaint plaza.

- ❑ Enjoy the sites from a horse-drawn carriage. You'll have time to study impressive building architecture, the kids will love the clop-clop-clop on the cobblestone, and the horse will earn its oats for the night. 2004 prices: €30 per carriage for a 45-minute ride. (Wouldn't be caught dead in a horse drawn carriage? Use the time to explore on your own.)

❑   Shop Calle Sierpes and the parallel streets of Cuna and Velázquez for traditional Spanish hats, fans, castanets, and ceramics. (Allow one hour)

Food tips: Looking for a french fry break? McDonald's and Burger King are located at the far end of Calle Sierpes on Alfonso XII.

Looking for a taste of home? The Texas Lone Star Saloon is located near the Cathedral at Placentines 25. To get there, exit the Cathedral via the orange tree patio, turn right onto Alemanes and left onto Placentines, and the restaurant will be on your right.

Big news in 2004! Starbucks opened a shop in a prime Sevilla location! You can find it and a cold Frappachino on the corner of Almanes and Avenida de la Constitution opposite the cathedral.

Highlight: The carriage ride, an excellent way to view the city. We were able to see the major sites without having to walk for miles, and our toddler *loved* watching the horse.

Lowlight: Discovering a lovely, embroidered, silk scarf was close to 200 euros. That was just more than I wanted to pay.

Sidelight: If you visit Sevilla on a Sunday, go in the morning to witness the incredible animal street market. Open from about 8:00–14:00, you can find birds and an eclectic mix of other animals for sale at the Plaza de la Alfalfa. Have a taxi take you directly there, or on foot from the Cathedral head up Calle Alvarez Quintero four or five blocks and bear to the right, then follow the crowds and noise.

Hint: If you are headed to Sevilla to shop, plan accordingly. While some shops buck the traditional Spanish schedule, many are closed Saturday afternoon, Sunday, and during afternoon siesta.

Directions: Take the train. From the El Puerto de Santa María train station you can relax and take in the countryside on the trip. Trains leave almost hourly to Sevilla. Check out www.renfe.es/ingles for timetables and prices. To get downtown from the Sevilla station, take a taxi to the cathedral, take the bus (check the information booth inside the train station for schedules), or walk.

If you are walking, you need a map of the city. Pick one up at the train station information booth. In general, exit the train station on the taxi-stand side, bear right, and head down Juan Antonio Cavestany. Turn right onto Avenida de Luis Montoto, left on Menendez Pelayo, and right on San Fernando. Turn right onto Avenida de la Constitución at the Puerta de Jerez. The Cathedral will be on your right in a few blocks.

If you decide you want to drive to Sevilla, it takes about one hour 20 minutes to reach the city center and park. On the A-4 you'll pay a toll on the way up and the way back, 2004 prices: €5 each way. From Rota, drive towards Jerez on the A-491. At the casino/water park traffic circle take the 2:00 exit towards El Portal (CA-201). In six miles (10 km), when the road comes to a 'T' at a traffic circle, turn right onto the A-381. In one mile (1.6 km), take the A-4 north to Sevilla. Travel about 52 miles (84 km) on the A-4 and take the first Sevilla city center exit you see before crossing the Guadalquivir River on a bridge. Follow the signs to the city center and look for a parking garage. If you miss the first city center exit you'll see many more off the A-4. If you follow the way we drove in, you will drive about two miles (three km) from the A-4 exit, turn left at the large stadium, Estadio Manuel Ruiz de Lopera, drive about one mile (1.6 km) passing the Parque de María Luisa on your right, turn right at the traffic circle onto Avenida de Roma, and look for an underground parking structure straight ahead. On a Sunday, driving through the city and locating parking was manageable, but I wouldn't attempt it on a weekday.

Sevilla Travel Notes:

Sevilla II

Sevilla Day Two highlights the Alcázar, the old Moorish palace still in use by Spain's Royal Family. This is a gorgeous palace with extensive gardens and shouldn't be missed. The rest of the day features free sightseeing so you can save your money for *tapa* hopping and all of the ceramics you can carry home.

Travel time: By train, from the El Puerto de Santa María station to the Sevilla-Santa Justa station, one hour 10 minutes to one hour 20 minutes depending on your train, plus a 15-minute taxi ride or 45-minute walk into the center of town. If driving, it takes about one hour 20 minutes.

Things to do in a day:

- ❏ Spend your morning looking up at intricate ceilings and admiring extensive gardens of the Alcázar. Be aware that descriptive signs providing information are sparse; so if you want more details on the Alcázar, rent the audio guide. Open on Tuesday–Saturday from 9:30–17:00, and Sunday from 9:30–13:30. Extended hours in the summer. Closed Monday. 2004 prices: €5. (Allow 1.5 hours to wander without the audio guide)

- ❏ Wind your way through the narrow streets of the Santa Cruz Barrio, the old Jewish quarter. Don't forget to tear your gaze away from all of the pottery stores and look up at the great wrought-iron balconies teaming with plants and flowers. (Allow 30+ minutes)

- ❏ Walk through the Plaza de España and the impressive building built for the 1929 Ibero-American Exhibition. Relax on a tile bench representing your favorite Spanish province (listed alphabetically from left to right) and take in the amazing architecture and huge fountain. (Allow 30+ minutes)

❑   Wander through the Parque de María Luisa. There are trees, plants, fountains, birds, an occasional grassy area, and even some playground equipment to make the kids happy. (Allow one hour or more to explore)

Food tip: Choose from many cafes and restaurants in the Santa Cruz district. Enjoy *tapas* or lunch here where the prices range from rather expensive to fairly reasonable tourist prices. The outdoor cafes located in charming, small plazas tend to be on the "rather expensive" side. For lower prices, venture out of the plazas into narrow, little restaurants located on narrow, little streets.

Highlight: The Alcázar palace is gorgeous, and not at all crowded if you tour it on Christmas Eve.

Lowlight: Unless you rent an audio guide, there's no map provided for the Alcázar. You will need to rely on a keen sense of direction to guide you through the intricate maze of rooms.

Sidelight: A scene in *Star Wars Episode II: Attack of the Clones* was filmed at Sevilla's Plaza de España. Check out Chapter 15 on the DVD when Anakin and Senator Amidala return to Naboo.

Hint: Sevilla Day Two features quite a bit of walking. Wear comfortable walking shoes.

Directions: Take the train. From the El Puerto de Santa María train station you can relax and take in the countryside on the trip. Trains leave almost hourly to Sevilla. Check out www.renfe.es/ingles for timetables and prices. To get downtown from the Sevilla station, take a taxi to the Alcázar, take the bus (check the information booth inside the train station for schedules), or walk (see Sevilla I, the Alcázar is next to the cathedral). If you decide you want to drive, see Sevilla I for directions.

Sevilla Travel Notes:

Sevilla III

Head back to Sevilla to see some of the sites you didn't have time to visit on Day One or Two. This city has so much to offer. After all, as long as it's not sweltering, any day spent in Sevilla is a good day.

Travel time: By train, from the El Puerto de Santa María station to the Sevilla-Santa Justa station, one hour 10 minutes to one hour 20 minutes depending on your train, plus a 15-minute taxi ride or a 45-minute walk into the center of town. If driving, it takes about one hour 20 minutes.

Things to do in a day:

❏ Visit the Torre del Oro (Tower of Gold). What was once a Moorish defensive tower is now a Naval museum. The museum features ship models, old maps, and paintings of important sea captains from Spain's naval history. The upper windows have views of the river.

Open on Tuesday–Friday from 10:00–14:00, and on Saturday, Sunday, and holidays from 11:00–14:00. Closed Monday. 2004 prices: €1. Tuesday free. (Allow 15 minutes)

❑ Take a stroll from the Torre del Oro to the Isabel II Bridge, also known as the Triana Bridge. Walk along the river for atmosphere, or up on the street for architecture. Pop into the bullring museum if you haven't visited the Ronda bullring yet. (Allow 15–20 minutes to walk to the bridge)

❑ Wander and shop through the narrow streets of Triana. Historically, Triana was the ceramics district. Today you will find old buildings covered with elaborate tiles. What you won't find are ceramic stores and studios on every street corner. If you are looking to buy ceramics, turn right at the plaza after crossing the Triana Bridge, and one block down you will find a few shops. (Allow 30+ minutes to explore the streets)

❑ Visit the Museo de las Bella Artes, a fine art museum considered second in Spain only to Madrid's El Prado. The museum features primarily religious art located in an old convent. The convent alone is worth a visit. It has courtyards, fountains, and a cross-shaped chapel with a painted dome ceiling. Open on Tuesday from 15:00–20:00; Wednesday–Saturday from 9:00–20:00; and Sunday from 9:00–14:00. Closed Monday. 2004 prices: €1.50. (Allow one hour)

Food tip: There are restaurants and cafés lining the river on Betis Street in the Triana district. The setting can't be beat. Find a casual café and enjoy the refreshing gazpacho. Ours was served in a tall glass with ice for sipping. *Pijotas* was listed on the menu as an Andalucían fried fish specialty. I ordered it and found out it's a small white-fleshed fish presented in its entirety: head, tail, fins, and skin.

Highlight: Eating along the Guadalquivir River, shaded by an umbrella on a sunny day, with an excellent gazpacho appetizer.

Lowlight: We did quite a lot of walking and backtracking in the hot sun. If you are interested in the sidelight river cruise, do it right after visiting the Torre del Oro to avoid unnecessary backtracking.

Sidelight: If you don't mind a touristy experience, take a one-hour river cruise on the Guadalquivir River. Embark next to the Torre del Oro for a tour. Departures are every 30 minutes. Cruises are offered from 11:00–22:00. Unfortunately, after finally convincing my husband he would survive such a tourist trap, we discovered tickets were 13 euros and they didn't take credit cards. Thirteen euros for a one-hour river cruise? We decided to pass, but those with deeper pockets may enjoy it.

Hint: There are many other sites to see in Sevilla. You may enjoy the Hospital de la Caridad, Hospital de los Venerables Sacerdotes, Casa de Pilatos, or the Museo Arqueológico. Pick up a city guide to discover all of the possibilities.

Directions: Take the train. From the El Puerto de Santa María train station you can relax and take in the countryside on the trip. Trains leave almost hourly to Sevilla. Check out www.renfe.es/ingles for timetables and prices. To get downtown from the Sevilla station, take a taxi to the Torre del Oro, take the bus (check the information booth inside the train station for schedules), or walk (the Torre del Oro is next to the river). If you decide you want to drive, see Sevilla I for directions.

Sevilla Travel Notes:

Tangier, Morocco

Morocco, in a word, is exotic. It is a land of old and new, full of color and camels, and flavored with spices like cinnamon and saffron. Tangier, the closest port town to Spain, can be reached in less than three hours from the Rota area and should be seen at least once. But pack your sense of adventure; you are entering a third world country. On your tour of the exotic you can expect to be hurried, hassled, hustled, and herded. But go anyway—the sights and sounds of North Africa await.

The easiest way to visit Morocco is to see your favorite travel agent first. Book a one-day or two-day tour leaving from Tarifa going to Tangier (or Tanger in Spanish), Morocco. We were able to make all the arrangements mid-week for a weekend trip in the spring. Currently, the ferry company FRS runs tours, and information can be found on the web at www.frs.es. In 10 minutes, the travel agent was able to book our passage, confirm our show time, and take our payment. This is the easiest way to get there. If the idea of a package tour leaves a bad taste in your mouth, and a little intimidation doesn't bother you (trust me, there *is* an intimidation factor when first arriving in Morocco) then see the do-it-yourself section on how to do it alone.

Travel time: About three hours. One hour 30 minutes to arrive in Tarifa; five minutes to check-in at the ferry terminal; five minutes to re-park, clean everything out of the interior of your car, and put it into the trunk; five minutes to walk back to the port; 30 minutes waiting time; and 35–45 minutes for the ferry to reach Tangier.

Things to do on your one-day tour:

- ❏ Get on the tour bus for a ride to the sites.

- ❏ Walk from the Kasbah area through the medina (market). Watch for snake charmers, musicians, and dancers near the Kasbah and fresh fruit, freshly baked bread, and live chickens in the market. (1 hour)

- ❏ Eat lunch in a relaxing restaurant while listening to live Moroccan music with voices, stringed instruments, and drums. (1+ hours)

- ❏ Stop at the "art school" to learn about Moroccan carpets and meet quite a few carpet salesmen. (<1 hour)

- ❏ Stop at the spice shop. Get an offering of perfumed soap, food spices, creams for wrinkles, "natural aphrodisiacs", sinus problem cures, headache cures, and henna, a natural vegetable dye for your hair. (<30 minutes)

- ❏ Have a drink on the terrace of the Continental Hotel. Check inside for a little bazaar where you don't have to negotiate for prices. (30 minutes)

- ❏ Take a short bus tour of the new city. (30 minutes)

- ❏ Stop for the obligatory camel photo shoot. (15 minutes)

- ❏ Get dropped off at the harbor at 15:00 to catch your 16:00 ferry.

Things to do the next day on your two-day tour:

- ❏ Hire a local guide. Our FRS guide recommended a man named Hassan to us. He often works outside the Chellah Hotel, but no doubt he would be willing to meet you wherever you are. He can be reached at 00 (212) 68-38-0658 from Spain, or 068-38-0658 from within Morocco. He didn't ask for a set price. We paid him 10 euros an hour with a generous tip because it was raining and because we didn't buy a carpet.

- ❑ Ask your guide to see the town. Inquire about good photo spots in the old city. See the covered marketplace and an upstairs area where people work their looms. Look for anything specific you would like to buy.

- ❑ Go to another "art school" carpet store. It doesn't matter who you use as your guide; they will all take you to a carpet store, but the setting will probably be a little more relaxed than the day before.

- ❑ Ask your guide questions about Morocco: its people, its government, and their economy. You will learn a lot in conversation with a local.

- ❑ Walk back to your hotel to gather your luggage, eat lunch, and wait for the tour bus to bring you to the port.

Food tip: If you have never tasted Moroccan food, you're in for a treat. On the package tour, the restaurant and menu will already be chosen for you, but here are some examples of some of the food you may experience during your brief stay in Morocco.

The bread served here is generally a thick flatbread, made with leavening and served in flat, round loaves. There are a variety of soups served. Harira is a lamb stew made with lamb, lentils, barley, tomatoes, celery, and flavored with cinnamon and chili pepper flakes. It is often served after sunset during Ramadan. A salad you might try is a marinated and chopped cucumber, tomato, and onion salad.

Kebabs are a typical food of North Africa. They might be served as an appetizer or a main course. Try the melt-in-your-mouth saffron-flavored chicken kebabs or the spiced ground lamb loaded onto metal skewers and cooked over an open flame. In either case, they'll be good.

The quintessential Moroccan meal is chicken or lamb *tagine*. It's often cooked with onions, potatoes, and perhaps dates or raisins in an earthenware pot with a conical shaped lid that traps all of the juices and flavors. It's served over a bed of couscous, a fine wheat-based grain that looks like grains of sand. Wrap up your meal with a flaky pastry coated in honey and a glass of sweet mint tea. You'll not walk away hungry.

Highlight: Being in exotic North Africa with the music, the charmers, the dancers, and the food within a few hours of Rota.

Lowlight: A six-hour tour through a port city with a population of two million just doesn't feel like authentic Morocco. That being said, in 1995 on a two-week camping tour through the Moroccan deserts and mountains, my brother and I also saw snake charmers and dancers, ate Moroccan food to Moroccan music, rode camels, and visited a carpet store and spice shop. It just didn't feel as canned.

Sidelight: If you feel that the rest of Morocco is at your feet, consider a two-week guided tour through the country, or go it alone. My favorite city is Fez with its narrow streets that twist through the huge medina, upstairs views of the leather tanning pits, and sauntering donkeys, the preferred method of transportation, negotiating the streets with their loads and riders.

Other places you may visit are the capital city of Rabat, the Roman ruins at Volubilis, the holy city Moulay that resembles a *pueblo blanco*, the rose-colored sand dunes of Erg Chebbi, the Meski Oasis, the Atlas Mountains, Todra Gorge with its lush green valley surrounded by dry brown desert, and Marrakech with its incredible market square filled with animals, performers, snake charmers, and a resident "dentist" (a gentleman with a card table filled with rows of pulled teeth). This is definitely a country with a lot of character.

Hints:

1. Bring your passport; you're going to a different continent. If you're in the military, you'll probably need to take leave.

2. Check the exchange rate before you go. Most merchants take euro, but may give change or quote prices in Moroccan dirham, and you'll want to know how much they're quoting for that copper teapot. In 2004, one euro was about 10 dirhams.

3. Wear conservative clothing. It's better not to show your knees or shoulders, as Morocco is predominantly a Muslim country.

4. Leave your Spanish dictionary at home and bring your French one. Most of Morocco was formerly a French colony, gaining independence in 1956.

5. Put sunscreen on before you leave the car and get on the ferry. There's not a lot of time for yourself once you disembark the ferry.

6. If you want a window seat on the ferry, get in line early at the ferry terminal.

7. Before you get off the ferry, make sure your day trip bag is packed with your day trip stuff and your camera is not packed in your overnight bag. (Live and learn.)

8. Before disembarking the ferry, you'll need to get your ferry pass or your passport stamped. If you are going for a day trip, you'll only have your ferry pass stamped. If you are staying overnight, you'll have your passport stamped. Look for a man sitting at a table on the ferry's upper deck to stamp these. If you get off the ferry without the stamp, the official at the end of the boat ramp will send you back.

9. Wear a money belt and keep your cell phone tucked out of sight.

10. Bring lots of euro change for tips. You should think about tipping the street performers, the waiters, the musicians, your guide, etc. Be generous.

11. Be cautious. Drink bottled water.

12. Our fellow travelers with a two-year old used a stroller for their daughter, but they had to carry it half of the time. Baby backpacks are the way to go!

13. If you indicate an interest in anything, expect to be hounded until you give in and buy it.

14. Bargain hard.

15. If you buy something and the next guy on the street offers you the same thing for one-third of the price you just paid, take comfort that you helped the local economy by paying extra.

16. Items that are offered for sale on the street include bracelets, small drums, teapots, and woven straw baskets. You should be able to get a better deal on the street than in the store for these items, but you won't

have a lot of time to bargain if you're with your tour group. You'll have to walk and negotiate prices at the same time.

17. Because most of us are western and don't know how to bargain, I offer this as a sampling of prices we were quoted in 2004: for a handmade wool carpet runner we didn't need, the price started at 700 euros and only came down to 600 euros. We didn't buy it. A metal-worked mirror started at 350 euros, and when it got down to 90 euros, it seemed like such a bargain we bought it. I know…we paid way too much. In the shop, a functional silver-colored teapot went for 20 euros, and on the street, a smaller, golden, decoration-only teapot went for 10 euros.

18. When departing Morocco after your two-day tour, you will get your passport stamped at the Gare Maritime Ouest building. Border authorities prefer that men get all the family passports stamped (Muslim cultural issues).

19. Tip the guide helping you get your passport stamped at the Maritime building. You may get onto the ferry faster.

20. If you have any Moroccan dirhams, get them changed at the port area before boarding for Spain. You are not supposed to leave the country with Moroccan money.

21. You may run into a man at the port selling woven straw bags. Before brushing him off, you might consider buying one. They make a convenient, sturdy bag to carry your purchases. He should settle for two or three euros, but the woman who offered him only 50 euro-cents didn't go home with one.

The do-it-yourself tour: If we went a second time to Tangier, we would consider one of two options. The budget option is to take the ferry over and stay at a mid-range hotel. We liked the location of the Hotel Continental, 00 (212) 39-93-1024, and their set-price bazaar. The necessary steps are to book the ferry, book the hotel, take a taxi to the hotel, and hire a local guide. The luxury option is to stay at the five-star hotel, El Minzah, in the new part of town (www.elminzah.com). The necessary steps are to book the ferry, book the hotel, wait for their shuttle bus (possibly having to call repeatedly to check on its whereabouts while brushing off overly ambitious taxi drivers), hire a local guide, and enjoy a massage and mud bath in the hotel's spa at the end of the day.

Directions: From Rota, take the A-491 to the El Paseo mall traffic circle. Take the 3:00 exit on the N-IV towards Algeciras. In about 11 miles (18 km) follow the A-48/E-5 towards Algeciras. About 71 miles (114 km) from Rota turn right to Tarifa. In one mile (1.6 km), turn right at the old city wall. Take an immediate left and drive 0.2 miles (0.3 km) into the harbor parking lot. Check in at the desk at the Puerto de Tarifa building.

To re-park your car, exit the harbor parking lot and turn right. Take an immediate right, staying outside the city walls, and drive 0.2 miles (0.3 km). Park in the free, unsecured parking lot on the right. Go back into the Puerto de Tarifa building to get on the ferry.

After disembarking in Tangier, you will go through passport control (an official at the end of the ferry ramp), and be led onto a tour bus.

Tangier Travel Notes:

Tarifa

Tarifa, famous for its winds, is a historical city that guards the strait between the Mediterranean and the Atlantic. A mecca for windsurfers, this city also has a lot to offer the rest of us. The old city walls surround quaint cobblestone streets and the castle ramparts offer fabulous views across the sea to Morocco. Visit this city for its history or its culture and then stock up on some cool surfing gear.

Travel time: About one hour 30 minutes.

Things to do in a day:

- ❑ Visit the Iglesia de San Mateo (Church of Saint Matthew). The church is open daily from 9:00–13:00 and from 17:30–21:00. Free. (Allow 15 minutes)

- ❑ Explore the castle, Castillo de Guzmán El Bueno. Charged with defending the city, Guzmán El Bueno is the unfortunate one whose son was captured by the Moors in 1294. Instead of surrendering the castle, he surrendered his son and threw down his own knife for the Moors to use. His son's throat was slit with that same knife, but the castle was spared, and seven centuries later Guzmán is still a hero, and still called good. Open from 11:00–14:00 and 18:00–20:00. Closed Sunday afternoon and all day Monday. 2004 prices: €1.80 for adults and €0.60 for children. Buy your ticket at the small magazine and trinket shop across the street. (Allow one hour if you follow the guided path and climb the ramparts for sensational views)

- ❑ Stroll up Paseo Alameda. This is a pretty walk with a playground for kids, cafés for a drink, and a very busy Tourist Information Office. Stop in for a map or a pamphlet on your next adventure sport.

❑   Walk around the old city walls, through the old city gate, the Puerta de Jerez, and wander about on the narrow cobblestone streets. You'll find international visitors, surf shops, and plenty of atmosphere.

Food tip: The great thing about an international city is the international food. If you look hard enough, you should be able to find food to suit anyone's taste. We found Spanish, Italian, and Greek restaurants, and a little sushi and flamenco bar. We didn't eat at any of these because on the way into town I spotted the Tex-Mex restaurant we ended up at. It's located on the main street, Batalla del Salado, on your right as you drive into town and about half a block before you reach the old city walls. The nachos were tasty, the fajitas were authentic, and the atmosphere was pleasant. I'd definitely go back.

Highlight: We actually had a lot of fun stomping around the old castle, and the views from the top were of the port, the Med, and North Africa.

Lowlight: Looking like frazzled tourists as we raced from our car to Saint Matthew's Church because we were afraid of missing the visiting hours. Whew! We barely made it.

Sidelight: Tarifa is a city full of adventurous sidelights. At the Tourist Information Office you can pick up pamphlets on numerous excursions and adventure sports. Here's a listing of a few to get you started.

- For whale and dolphin watching try the Foundation for Information and Research on Marine Mammals at www.firmm.org, Whale Watch España at www.whalewatchtarifa.org, or Turmares at www.turmares.com.

- For windsurfing or kitesurfing rentals and lessons try Tarifa Spin Out at www.tarifaspinout.com.

- There are camping sites near Tarifa located off the A-48/E-5. Check out Camping Paloma at www.campingpaloma.com or Camping Tarifa at www.camping-tarifa.com.

- Last but not least, if you're a bird watcher, pick up information at the Tourist Information Office on the Route of Bird Observatories of Gibraltar.

Hint: Expect wind. Due to Tarifa's position next to the Strait of Gibraltar, the west wind, *Poniente*, and the east wind, *Levante*, buffet the city and coast with great strength. It is reported to be calm here less than 10 percent of the time. Either use a lot of hairspray, or expect to look windblown.

Directions: From Rota, take the A-491 to the El Paseo mall traffic circle. Take the 3:00 exit on the N-IV towards Algeciras. In about 11 miles (18 km) follow the A-48/E-5 towards Algeciras. About 71 miles (114 km) from Rota, turn right to Tarifa. In one mile (1.6 km), turn right at the old city wall. Take an immediate left and drive 0.2 miles (0.3 km) to the traffic light just before the harbor parking lot. Turn left, and then take an immediate right, staying outside the city walls. Drive 0.2 miles (0.3 km) and park in the free, unsecured, parking lot on the right.

Tarifa Travel Notes:

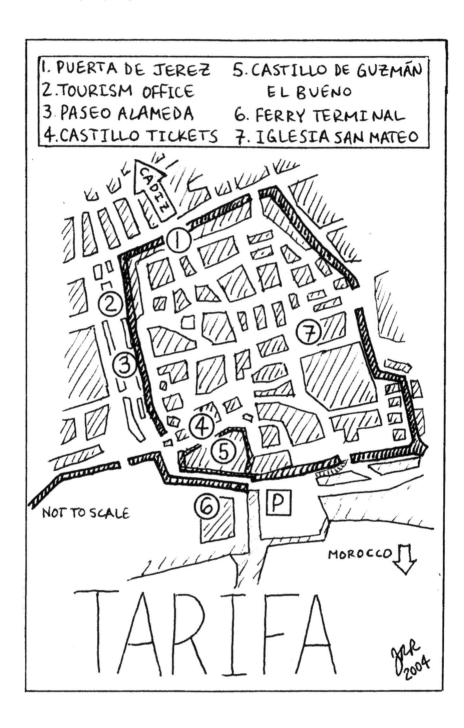

1. PUERTA DE JEREZ
2. TOURISM OFFICE
3. PASEO ALAMEDA
4. CASTILLO TICKETS
5. CASTILLO DE GUZMÁN EL BUENO
6. FERRY TERMINAL
7. IGLESIA SAN MATEO

CADIZ

NOT TO SCALE

MOROCCO

TARIFA

Ubrique

Ubrique is a charming little town on the route of the *pueblos blancos* (white villages). The town lies in an enviable location, set in a valley and bordered by both the Sierra de Grazalema and Los Alcornocales Natural Parks. A bubbling mountain stream runs right through the center of town. Of course this is not the only reason to visit. For centuries Ubrique has been producing leather goods, and today you can find a multitude of specialty leather stores. Handcrafted in workshops hidden in the old part of town, this leather is art.

Travel time: About one hour 30 minutes.

Things to do in a day:

- ❑ Shop for leather jackets.
- ❑ Shop for leather belts.
- ❑ Shop for leather gloves.
- ❑ Shop for leather luggage.
- ❑ Shop for leather shoes.
- ❑ Shop for leather wallets.
- ❑ Shop for leather purses.
- ❑ Shop for leather vests.
- ❑ Shop for leather pants…well, maybe not.

Things to do during siesta or after your credit card hits its limit:

- ❑ Walk through the old town of Ubrique.
- ❑ See the main plaza, La Plaza, bordered by a church and the town hall.

❑   Look up at the distinctive church, San Antonio, whose façade towers over much of Ubrique.

❑   Wander though narrow streets that resemble staircases: Fuentezuela, Guindaleta, Sanjurjo, and Saucos.

❑   Hike up to the *mirador* (lookout) for a bird's eye view of the city.

Food tip: For the best view in town, eat at Restaurante Plaza, located at the new bullring, Nueva Plaza de Toros, on Avenida Jesulín de Ubrique, s/n. This second story restaurant has panoramic views, dishes flavored with lots of garlic, and an exceptionally rich chocolate mousse.

Highlight: Heading to Ubrique for a leather belt and coming home with a belt, two purses, and a beautiful lambskin suede jacket.

Lowlight: The arrival of the credit card bill three weeks later.

Sidelight: If you arrive in Ubrique looking for more than lunch and leather, talk to someone from the Tourist Information Office. They can give you information on a little history, hiking, or both. For history, get info on Ocuri, the Roman ruins that lie one kilometer outside of town. For hiking, get information about the free access walk from Ubrique, through the Sierra de Grazalema Natural Park, to the next white village, Benaocaz. For both history and hiking, there are Paseos con Historia (walks through history) organized by the Information Office through the old town.

Hint: Make sure you arrive in town before 14:00. We didn't see a single leather shop open during siesta—luckily for our wallet's sake.

Directions: From Rota, drive towards Jerez on the A-491. At the casino/water park traffic circle take the 2:00 exit towards El Portal (CA-201). In six miles (10 km), when the road comes to a 'T' at a traffic circle, turn right onto the A-381. In one mile (1.6 km), take the A-4 north to Sevilla. In three miles (five km) take the A-382 exit. Turn right towards Arcos de la Frontera. Drive about 15 miles (24 km) and go straight through a number of stoplights. Central Arcos will be on your right. Just past Arcos, turn right onto the A-372. Signs point to Ubrique and El Bosque. Follow the A-372 approximately 17 miles (27 km). Turn right onto the A-373 following the signs to Ubrique. Travel eight miles (13 km) to reach the town. At the first traffic circle (more like a traffic triangle at a 'T' inter-section) turn right. Drive 0.1 miles (0.1 km) and turn right at the next traffic cir-cle (traffic triangle) onto the tree-lined street, Doctor Solis Pascual. Take the first right onto Doctor Zarco Bohorquez. There is a dirt parking lot in 0.1 miles (0.1 km) at the end of the street.

Leather shopping is located on Doctor Solis Pascual, Avenida España, and var-ious side streets. The Tourist Information Office is located at the far end of Doc-tor Solis Pascual, just over the small bridge crossing the stream and on the right hand side.

The new bullring, where the restaurant is located, can be seen up on a hill from most of the town. Coming from Rota on the A-373, before reaching the main part of town, take the first right onto Algeciras, then right on Granada, and left on Sebastián Macias El Pato. The bullring is located next to a commercial center.

Ubrique Travel Notes:

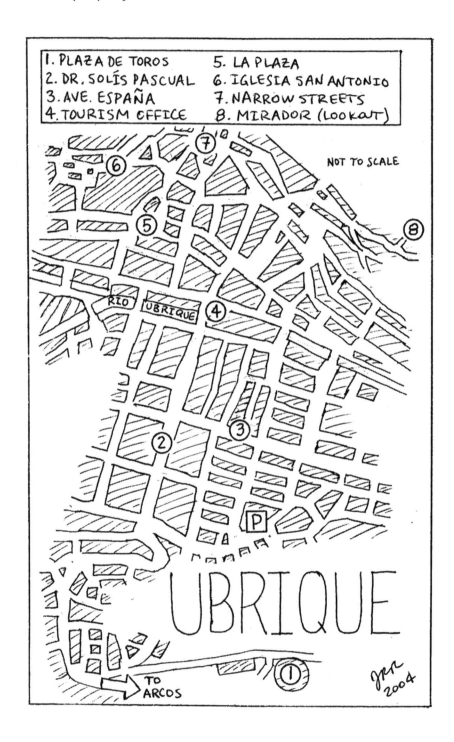

1. PLAZA DE TOROS
2. DR. SOLÍS PASCUAL
3. AVE. ESPAÑA
4. TOURISM OFFICE
5. LA PLAZA
6. IGLESIA SAN ANTONIO
7. NARROW STREETS
8. MIRADOR (LOOKOUT)

NOT TO SCALE

RIO UBRIQUE

P

UBRIQUE

TO ARCOS

jrr 2004

Vejer de la Frontera

Vejer de la Frontera is a historic village located south of Cadiz near the Atlantic Ocean. The unique feeling of the city stems from the fortress walls that enclose the old part of the city, still intact to this day. Consider Vejer de la Frontera as a day trip to take if you have a Monday holiday. The attraction of Vejer is the city itself, not any major tourist attractions that always seem to be closed on Mondays.

Travel time: About one hour.

Things to do in a day:

❑ Wander through the walled sections of Vejer and beyond to discover a remarkable city, one whose fortress walls were used as protection against Barbary Pirates. Be sure to see the major highlights (allow 2 hours):

- The church, Iglesia del Divino Salvador.
- The castle.
- The *mirador* (lookout) located outside the old city gate Arco de Puerta Cerrada.
- The Plaza de España located outside the old city gate Arco de la Villa.

Food tips: If you parked in the parking lot at the base of the hill, there's a restaurant that can be found on your way to or from the historic part of the city. Restaurante La Posada, located at Avenida Los Remedios 19, serves local cuisine featuring fish, pork, and lamb. Heads up—if you order the leg of lamb, you pretty much get the whole leg.

Located at the Plaza de España is a little shop named La Barbateña that sells preserved, smoked, and salted fish (www.selectosdebarbate.com). Barbate, the small seaside village near Vejer, has a fishing tradition originating with the Phoenicians and Romans. Even if you are not exactly sure what to serve with jars of preserved fish, it makes for a unique souvenir from the town.

Highlight: Winding through the narrow cobblestone streets and coming upon a vista overlooking the sparkling Atlantic with Morocco clearly in view.

Lowlight: Finding the first four restaurants we visited closed—it was January and off-season.

Sidelight: On your trip south you will be driving through a natural park area. The estuaries and salt flats that border the Bay of Cádiz are normally teeming with bird-life. In the winter you can expect to see wild ducks, storks, and gulls. In the summer you may get lucky and see wild flamingos.

Hint: If you like exploring, you really won't need a map. We discovered most of the interesting sights in the city on our own, just by wandering through the city.

Directions: From Rota, take the A-491 to the El Paseo mall traffic circle. Take the 3:00 exit on the N-IV towards Algeciras. In about 11 miles (18 km) follow the A-48/E-5 towards Algeciras. After about 22 miles (35 km) on the E-5 turn right towards Vejer de la Frontera. Turn left at the traffic circle onto the CA-214 and follow signs to Vejer. In just over one mile (1.6 km) you will come to a convenient pay parking area on your left. There is also street parking around the next traffic circle and up the street. Walk uphill and follow signs to the city center. City maps are available from the tourist services building in the park located next to the pay parking lot; so grab one before you head up into the city.

Vejer de la Frontera Travel Notes:

1. TOURISM OFFICE
2. PARQUE (PARK)
3. RESTAURANTE LA POSADA
4. ARCO DE LA SEGUR
5. IGLESIA (CHURCH)
6. ARCO DE LAS MONJAS
7. MIRADOR
8. ARCO DE PUERTA CERRADA
9. CASTILLO (CASTLE)
10. ARCO DE LA VILLA
11. PLAZA DE ESPAÑA
12. ARCO DE SANCHO IV

TO CADIZ

NOT TO SCALE

VEJER
DE LA FRONTERA

2004

Vila Real de Santo António, Portugal

Vila Real de Santo António is a great little city just over the Spain-Portugal border. This is the place to buy your cotton tablecloths and hand or beach towels and the closest spot to dive into delicious Portuguese food.

Travel Time: About two hours 45 minutes with a quick rest stop.

Things to do in a day:

- ❑ Stroll along the cobblestone sidewalk next to the river, Río Guadiana.

- ❑ Shop on the pedestrian streets. Many stores are even open during siesta if you arrive late into town.

- ❑ See the large plaza in the center of the pedestrian streets. You will often find a local street market here.

- ❑ Buy an inexpensive, quality, colorful tablecloth. 2003 prices: €10.

- ❑ Eat Portuguese food!

Food tip: Try the *bife à Portuguesa* (beefsteak Portuguese style), or some flavorful grilled fish. Chicken *Piri Piri* comes with a fiery sauce, and *cataplana* is a Portuguese specialty, meat or seafood cooked in a large, shell-shaped, copper pan with a hinged lid. Presentation is everything!

Highlight: Buying homemade desserts from a street vendor in the central plaza. She used delicious family recipes that were handed down to her by her grandmother.

Lowlight: Getting caught in freeway traffic leaving Sevilla towards Portugal on El Rocio pilgrimage weekend. The El Rocio pilgrimage honors the Virgin of El

Rocio and attracts around one million people each year. The actual date of the El Rocio pilgrimage varies each year, but it's held on the days surrounding Pentecost Sunday, about 50 days after Easter. Lesson learned: while some pilgrims travel by foot, horse, or cart across Doñana National Park to reach El Rocio, the majority of people travel by car by way of Sevilla.

Sidelight: While the rest of the Southern Portugal coast is really too far to be called a day trip, many people spend a weekend exploring the area. Albufeira is packed with English tourists and English pubs; Portimão has gorgeous beaches with interesting rock formations; Lagos has a great pedestrian shopping area with many cafes and ceramic shops; Ponto de Sagres and Cabo de São Vicente are considered "the end of the world" and have vistas from towering cliffs jutting out over the water; and a tiny beach cove, Praia da Beliche, located in-between the capes is worth the 156 stairs to see the incredibly blue water.

Hint: The sweater vendors at Capo São Vincente won't bargain on prices, just ask my husband.

Directions: From Rota, drive towards Jerez on the A-491. At the casino/water park traffic circle take the 2:00 exit towards El Portal (CA-201). In six miles (10 km), when the road comes to a 'T' at a traffic circle, turn right onto the A-381. In one mile (1.6 km), take the A-4 north to Sevilla, and when you reach Sevilla, take the E-1/A-49 towards Huelva and Portugal. It takes about two hours 30 minutes to get to the suspension bridge at the Portugal border. After the bridge, travel about one mile (1.6 km) to the Vila Real de Santo António exit, loop around, and turn right towards Vila Real de Santo António. Travel about 2.5 miles (four km) to the "V. Real" sign and turn left towards the river. Follow that road and in less than one mile (one km) you will bear right and the road will become a cobblestone street bordering the river. Head towards the marina where there is lots of street parking and quite a few tour buses. If you miss the "V. Real" sign, you can get to the city center by going into town. Drive towards the city center and left towards the river and marina. You can find parking in a corner lot across from the beginning of the pedestrian street.

Vila Real de Santo António Travel Notes:

Zahara de la Sierra

Zahara de la Sierra is one of the *pueblos blancos* (white villages), perched on a hill in the region of Sierra de Grazalema Natural Park. The drive to Zahara offers outstanding views of both the village and the bordering reservoir. Have fun today—picnic by the waterside, walk through the town, and storm the castle.

Travel time: Only 70 miles (113 km), but the trip takes about one hour 30 minutes if you include a 5-minute stop to buy hot *churros* from a stand in Arcos. It's about one hour 25 minutes to the picnic area plus five minutes to reach Zahara.

Things to do in a day:

- ❏ Enjoy a picnic next to the reservoir on a lazy afternoon. (About one hour, or at your leisure)

- ❏ Admire the main church in town and the plaza overlooking the rooftops. (Allow 15 minutes to walk to the church and 15+ minutes to enjoy the surroundings)

- ❏ Hike (uphill) to the Moorish castle (free access) and to its rooftop for incredible views of the surrounding foothills and reservoir. Follow the sign to the Villa Medieval. (Allow one hour, it *is* a bit of a hike)

Food tip: Early February is wild asparagus season! You can buy it in bunches from gentlemen standing on the side of the road approaching Zahara. We were given the shocking price of €15 for a large bunch, but it was the end of his day so we negotiated down to 10. Come to find out, that was a pretty good price. We actually saw numerous people hunting for wild asparagus up the hill from our picnic area. The flavor has been described as sharp, but I would lean more towards bitter. What to do with wild asparagus? Search the Internet for Spanish wild asparagus recipes, and then pass some asparagus out to your friends—you'll have plenty.

Highlight: The castle's cobblestone path offers great views and as a February bonus, was lined with colorful wildflowers and blossoms.

Lowlight: Nothing major: we forgot the picnic tablecloth, discovered slick cobblestones can be a little treacherous in the rain, and we couldn't tell you what lies at the very end of the Sendero de la Bodega (see sidelight).

Sidelight: The trail system of the Sierra de Grazalema Natural Park includes the Sendero de la Bodega, a semi-urban walk originating in Zahara. Authorization is not required, but you may have to ask a number of people where to find the trailhead. The trail starts at the lower part of the village, on the side opposite of the reservoir. There is a stone path that leads past the Pension Restaurante Los Tadeos, past the municipal swimming pool, and becomes a dirt trail leading you through the hillside olive groves. It was a pleasant hike in mild temperatures, but as the trail was muddy and rain was threatening, we didn't actually reach the end before turning around.

Hint: It's not a bad idea to bring a flashlight for the castle. The interior is not lighted and the stairways can be quite dark.

Directions: From Rota, drive towards Jerez on the A-491. At the casino/water park traffic circle take the 2:00 exit towards El Portal (CA-201). In six miles (10 km), when the road comes to a 'T' at a traffic circle, turn right onto the A-381. In one mile (1.6 km), take the A-4 north to Sevilla. In three miles (five km), take the A-382 exit. Turn right towards Arcos de la Frontera. Follow the A-382 for about 44 miles (71 km) and take the exit towards Zahara. Turn left at the stop onto the CA-531 to Zahara. In about three miles (five km) will be the Embalse de Zahara-El Gastor reservoir. Immediately before you cross the reservoir bridge there is a dirt road and a picnic area to the left (no signs). There are picnic tables next to the main road and further down the dirt road near the water. Park here to picnic.

After your picnic, continue on the CA-531 bordering the reservoir, and in one mile (1.6 km) turn right to Zahara. For the easiest parking follow this road about 1.4 miles (2.2 km) and turn right. Travel up the hill about 0.2 miles (0.3 km) and park in a small lot on the right. You will be on the far edge of town. It's possible to make an earlier right turn into the heart of town and look for the small parking garage, but it's certainly not the easier route.

After parking, walk along the main road through town to the old church and the plaza with the *mirador* (lookout). The road continues uphill towards the castle.

Zahara de la Sierra Travel Notes:

APPENDIX A

Rota Area Map

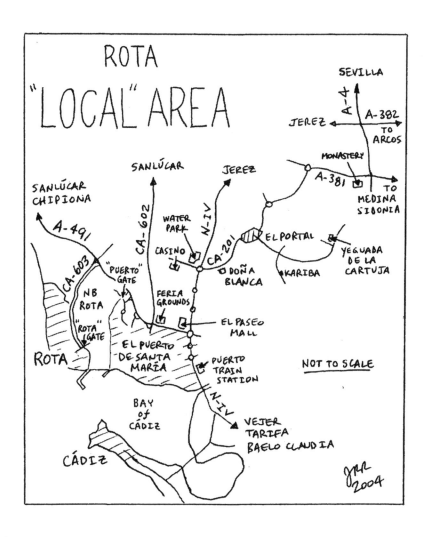

APPENDIX B

Traveler's Checklist

- ❑ Check forecast on the web
- ❑ Snacks, drinks, and bottled water
- ❑ Backpack to carry everything in
- ❑ Sunscreen
- ❑ Hats
- ❑ Sunglasses
- ❑ Passports for across the border and hotel stays
- ❑ Lip balm
- ❑ Insect repellant
- ❑ Guide book and pen
- ❑ Small medical kit for your car
- ❑ Check gas, oil, windshield washer fluid, and tire pressure if traveling by car
- ❑ Maps
- ❑ Emergency phone numbers
- ❑ Rain protection
- ❑ Mobile phone (remember to charge it)
- ❑ Camera and film
- ❑ Video camera (remember to charge it)

❑   Euro, traveler's checks and/or credit card

❑   Euro change for parking

If staying overnight:

❑   Hotel confirmation

❑   Bathing suit if hotel has a pool

If traveling with kids:

❑   Diapers and wipes

❑   Baby food

❑   Medicine

❑   Bath items

❑   Pajamas

❑   Toys and activity items

❑   Portable DVD player and videos (remember to charge it)

❑   Kid's music for the car

❑   Stroller or baby backpack

When leaving the house:

❑   Feed pets

❑   Water plants

❑   Check oven and stove

❑   Check that transformers are unplugged

❑   Lock doors and gates

❑   Check out if going on leave (military)

❑   Consider using timers for lights

APPENDIX C

Day Trip Recommendations

Day trips not to miss

Arcos de la Frontera (closest *pueblo blanco* to Rota with dramatic views)
Cordoba I (gorgeous city with heavy Moorish flavor)
El Portal—Yeguada de la Cartuja (thrilling horse show)
Gibraltar (cave and apes)
Granada (the Alhambra, an incredible Moorish fortress and palace)
Jerez II (horses and sherry)
Ronda (views from the old bridge)
Sevilla I (historic cathedral and tower)
Sevilla II (lovely Alcázar and Plaza de España)
Tangier, Morocco (exotic Africa)
Tarifa (historic city with a breezy attitude)

Day trips to do with kids

Cadiz II (ferry ride and parks)
Chipiona (beach)
Doñana National Park (ferry ride and animals)
El Portal—Kariba (crocodiles)
El Portal—Yeguada de la Cartuja (horse show)
Gibraltar (cable car ride, apes, and cave)
Jerez I (zoo)
Jerez II (horse show)
Laguna de Medina (easy hike)
La Rábida (old ships to explore)
Rota (beach and park)

Sevilla I (carriage ride)
Zahara de la Sierra (picnic by the water)

Day trips to experience the great outdoors

Antequera (hike through limestone formations)
Doñana National Park (bird and animal watching)
Doñana Natural Park (bird watching and hiking or biking)
El Bosque (hike)
Grazalema (hike and mountain views)
Laguna de Medina (easy hike around wetlands)
Olvera (Vía Verde bike route, see sidelight)

Day trips that won't cost an arm and a leg

Arcos de la Frontera
Baelo Claudia
Benalup—Casas Viejas
Chipiona
Doña Blanca
Doñana Natural Park
El Bosque
El Puerto de Santa María
Grazalema
Laguna de Medina
Medina Sidonia
Rota
Sanlúcar de Barrameda
Vejer de la Frontera
Zahara de la Sierra

Day trips that won't take your entire day

Baelo Claudia
Chipiona
Doña Blanca
Doñana National Park
Doñana Natural Park

El Portal—Kariba
El Portal—Yeguada de la Cartuja
El Puerto de Santa María
Italica
Laguna de Medina
Rota

0-595-34129-2

Made in the USA
Las Vegas, NV
27 November 2021

35350100R00097